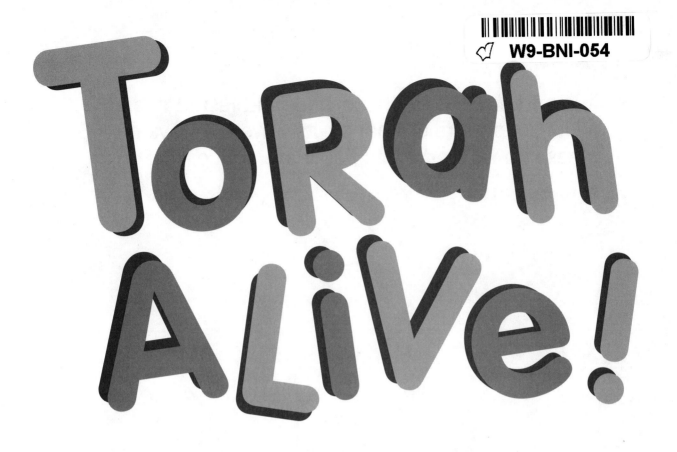

Torah ALive!

An Early Childhood Torah Curriculum

Parent Connection

Lorraine Posner Arcus

URJ Press

New York, New York

It is a tree of life for those who hold fast to it, and all its supporters are happy. Its ways are ways of pleasantness, and all its paths are peace.

Proverbs 3:18, 17

Design by Dahlia G. Schoenberg

This book is printed on acid-free paper.
Copyright © 2004 by URJ Press
Manufactured in the United States of America

10 9 8 7 6 5 4 3 2 1

CONTENTS

A Guide for Parents

As it is taught: The world is sustained solely through the breath of children when they are studying.

Babylonian Talmud, *Shabbat* 119b

GETTING STARTED

The Torah (תּוֹרָה) is God's great gift to the Jewish people. Through the study of Torah, the children learn a set of relevant values and are provided with the opportunity to discuss sensitive feelings and issues.

Torah study for the young child should be vibrant and exciting. The Torah is filled with wonderful lessons, fabulous personalities, and enthralling events. Young children love stories. This curriculum, based on developmentally appropriate experiences for young children and my personal experiences in the classroom, capitalizes on their love of lessons taught in "story" form.

Children learn by doing. By re-creating the lessons from the Torah through their own dramatization, young students make it their own. The children readily identify with the biblical figures, and the Torah comes alive as the children become active participants in the weekly Torah lessons. If we imbue in our children a love of Torah study and surround their classroom with pictorial and artistic representations of the Torah lesson, the children are likely to develop a sense of the Torah as an integral part of their everyday lives.

THE TORAH: SACRED WORDS

The Torah, the first five books of the Bible, is also called the Five Books of Moses. It is written in Hebrew, on a scroll of parchment. Each end of the Torah scroll is attached to a wooden roller, called *eitz chayim*

(עֵץ חַיִּים). The Torah scroll is kept in the *Aron Kodesh* (אֲרוֹן קֹדֶשׁ), the Holy Ark, within the synagogue or place of prayer. Each week, we read a new *parashah* (פָּרָשָׁה), portion of the Torah. We read the first chapter on Simchat Torah (שִׂמְחַת תּוֹרָה), right after we have read the last chapter, completing the yearly cycle. Every year, we start again from the beginning, learning something new each time we study a familiar lesson. The Torah is the basis of Judaism and is an important way to learn the ancient history of the Jews and the values through which we live our lives.

As preparation for embarking on Torah study, one may discuss the physical qualities of the Torah: the *eitz chayim*, the parchment, how a Torah is written, who writes a Torah, the *rimonim* (רִמּוֹנִים), or Torah crowns, when the Torah is read, where the Torah is kept, the difference between a Sephardic Torah and an Ashkenazic Torah. It is very exciting for children to see a "real" *sefer Torah* (Torah scroll). Every synagogue has Torah scrolls in the *Aron Kodesh*. Many synagogues provide stuffed toy Torah scrolls so young children can participate in the Torah procession, *hakafah* (הַקָּפָה), around the synagogue.

QUESTIONS: SACRED DISCUSSION

"The Torah has seventy faces," and we are invited to interpret it.

B'midbar Rabbah 13:15

Invite your children to ask their own questions. Young children are regarded by theologians as being some of the best students of Torah. Invite them to offer their interpretations. The open-ended discussions conducted at this age will be an introduction to the way Torah study is conducted throughout one's life. Create an atmosphere in which Torah study is an exploration and discussion, not just storytelling. Encourage your children to question and ponder the lessons from the Torah. Keep a chart or book of great questions asked by your children. The questions provided in this book, at the end of each lesson, are only a suggestion to be used as a springboard. When developing your own set of questions, be sure to include ones that are open-ended, sparking curiosity and critical thought, along with those questions that recall facts.

When asking factual questions, refer to the synopsis included in the chapter or the Torah text for correct answers. Questions suggested in this book that contain phrases such as "Why do you think . . . ?" or "What do you think . . . ?" may not necessarily have "correct" answers. Try to be accepting of all ideas. There are students and scholars who spend their lives discussing and answering some of these questions.

"DID THIS REALLY HAPPEN?"

Often children will ask, "Did this really happen?" A simple and accurate answer would be, "This is how it is written in the Torah." Every Torah is exactly the same. From this text, we learn lessons and values that guide our lives.

It is important to recognize that Jewish tradition doesn't portray any individual as being exclusively good. The personalities in the Bible were subject to human frailties, made mistakes, and may have used questionable judgment. We acknowledge their mistakes and learn from them. Additionally, the events in the lives of these leading biblical characters illustrate that despite mistakes, a person can still travel in the path of God.

APPROPRIATE LITERATURE

A bibliography has been provided that includes a list of suggested, developmentally appropriate books. This is certainly only a partial list of available age-appropriate literature. When selecting books that are not on the list, make sure they reflect a Jewish perspective on the Bible before sharing them with your children. For example, many children's books illustrate God as an old man. There are many ways to "see" and "feel" God. Through the beautiful creations in nature, Jews can see and feel God. A book ascribing a human form to God through illustrations would not be an appropriate choice and would limit your children's abilities to develop their own individual perspective. It is also important to make sure the books you choose remain true to the Torah text or the midrashic literature.

WHAT IS MIDRASH?

There are many events and stories in the Torah where we feel we may need to "fill in the gaps" or provide answers that are not directly addressed in the story. There is a wealth of stories, each called a midrash (מִדְרָשׁ), that were written over many years by the great Rabbis, scholars, or contemporary authors. These are stories that are not directly from the Torah but help to answer questions that may arise. They enhance the scenarios that seem to need more information. The story of Avraham and the idols is an example of midrash. The Torah does not tell us about Avraham as a child. This midrash was developed to help us understand Avraham more fully. Make sure when citing a midrash that your children are aware that the story is not contained in the Torah.

WHAT ABOUT THE WOMEN?

Children frequently ask, "Why aren't there any girls in this story?" or "Why does God talk to the men so much?" We can't change the contents of the stories from the Torah, but we can make sure to emphasize the critical role of the women. While we adults may have the desire to conjecture about the role of women who are not directly mentioned in the Torah lesson, we must be careful to remain true to the text and not to teach children anything they will need to "unlearn" at another point in their education. You may tell your children that there were certainly many members of the community who were present, yet not directly mentioned in the Torah. You may also mention that the events of the Torah happened a long time ago and that men and women had different roles than they do today, when women and men have equally important roles and jobs.

THE TORAH AND OUR CONTEMPORARY LIVES

Learning Torah is an ongoing process. We study Torah throughout our lives. Each time we study a passage or story, even if we have studied it before, we learn new insights, generate new questions, and find new ways to relate those teachings to our everyday lives.

In the course of the academic year, there will be times when either ordinary or extraordinary events will occur. Seize the opportunity to use teachings from the Torah to solve a problem or relate to something wonderful that has occurred. For example, a guest may come to visit your home. We learn from Avraham and Sarah how to treat our guests. Enjoy the process, become part of the process, and watch the Torah come alive!

How to Use the *Torah Alive! Parent Connection*

HOW TO USE THIS BOOK

The *Torah Alive! Parent Connection* contains much of the same background information as the teacher's guide, so parents will have the same information as the teacher. Both editions contain the same **Introduction** and **Synopsis** for each lesson. The **Discussion Questions** and **Related Activities** are parallel but different. Many of the questions and activities in the *Parent Connection* relate to the child's family or environment. Children may be encouraged to share with the class projects or discussions in which they engaged with their families. Each lesson includes the following:

- **Title** of the lesson in English, Hebrew, and transliteration (Hebrew sounds using English letters), as well as the verses in the Torah covered by the lesson.

- **Picture** of how the students' dramatization of the Torah story might look in a classroom.

- **Introduction:** Background information providing the context in which the story takes place.

- **Synopsis:** A brief summary of the Torah story upon which the narration is based.

- **Discussion Questions:** Some of these questions require factual recall. However, most of the questions are open-ended to encourage thoughtful discussions and insights. As you become comfortable with the curriculum, you will generate your own questions. Write them down, and add them to your book. Encourage your child to share great insights with the teacher and classmates.

- **Related Activities:** Suggested craft activities or group projects to enhance the lesson.

The following sections appear at the end of the book:

- **Appendixes** including instructions for a recipe and a list of useful Web sites for early childhood education and Torah study for young children and adults. The Web sites are particularly useful for teachers and parents who wish to gain greater insights into the Torah lessons.

- **Glossary of Hebrew Terms**, written in Hebrew characters, transliteration, and translation.

- **Bibliography and Resources** with suggested books to read when learning about various Torah personalities. The teachers have the same bibliography. Don't be concerned about reading the same book at home with your child as was read in class. Your child will enjoy the book even more the second and third time around, cuddled in your arms, and will enjoy telling you what's going to come next!

LESSONS 1 AND 2

Creation

בְּרֵאשִׁית

B'reishit

Genesis 1:1–2:3

INTRODUCTION

The story of Creation, the first *parashah* in the Torah, is read on Simchat Torah and the following Shabbat. A suggestion would be to time this lesson to begin during Sukkot (סֻכּוֹת) so the children are familiar with the Creation story in time for Simchat Torah. Continue the lessons by finishing the related activities after Simchat Torah.

My favorite way to introduce the story of Creation is to gather a variety of books on the subject and see how different artists interpret the same text. Often, the children ask, "How could this happen in a day?" "What about the dinosaurs?" A simple answer is, "There are many versions of the story of Creation. This is how the Torah teaches us about Creation."

B'reishit (בְּרֵאשִׁית) is the first word of the Torah, as well as the Hebrew title of Genesis, the first book in the Torah. The word *B'reishit* can be translated as "When [God] began [creating]. . . ." This *parashah* describes how, for the first time, God created all that there is in the world. We can see for ourselves, however, that God continues the miracles of "creating" all the time.

Using one of the many beautiful books suggested in the bibliography, the children learn that there was an order to Creation and that God was proud of all that was created. God even created a day for us to rest.

SYNOPSIS

When God began to create the heaven and the earth, there was chaos and darkness and only God's spirit moved throughout the emptiness.

God said, "Let there be light"; and there was light. God saw that the light was good and separated the light from the darkness. God called the light Day and the darkness Night. And there was evening and there was morning, a first day.

God said, "Let there be a separation of the waters, water below and heavens above." And it was so. God called the space between the waters Sky. And there was evening and there was morning, the second day.

God said, "Let the waters gather together so dry land may appear." And it was so. God called the dry land Earth and the waters Seas. And God saw that this was good. And God said, "Let the earth grow flowers, trees without fruit, trees with fruit, and all types of vegetation." And it was so. And God saw that this was good. And there was evening and there was morning, the third day.

God said, "Let there be great lights in the sky to separate day from night; they will set the times for days and years." And it was so. God made two great lights: the larger light, the sun, to shine in the day, and the smaller light, the moon and the stars, to shine at night. And God saw that this was good. And there was evening and there was morning, the fourth day.

God said, "Let there be fish in the water and the birds in the sky." And God saw that this was good. God blessed them, saying, "Be fertile and increase." And there was evening and there was morning, the fifth day.

God said, "Let there be every kind of animal on the earth." And it was so. And God saw that this was good. And God said, "Let us make man. They shall rule the fish, the birds, the cattle, the whole earth and all the animals." And God created man and woman in God's image. God blessed them and said, "Be fertile and increase. Fill the earth and rule all the animals." And it was so. And God saw all that had been created and found it very good. And there was evening and there was morning, the sixth day.

The heaven and earth were finished. God rested on the seventh day. God blessed the seventh day and declared it holy because God ceased from all the work of creation.

DISCUSSION QUESTIONS

God created the seventh day as a day of rest, Shabbat. What can our family do to make Shabbat special?

RELATED ACTIVITIES

Shabbat List

Generate a list of activities your family can do to make Shabbat different from the rest of the week. Try to do something from the list each week!

Creation Mobile

Using construction paper, a variety of other kinds of paper, or pictures from magazines, fashion one picture to represent each day of Creation. Cut out the pictures, and attach a string to the top of each one. Suspend each picture, at varying lengths, from a wire hanger.

LESSON 3

Adam and Eve

אָדָם וְחַנָּה
Adam V'Chavah

Genesis 2:4–3:24

INTRODUCTION

In *B'reishit*, we learn that God created people on the sixth day. We now take a closer look at the first two people God created. We also learn about God's love, following and breaking rules, and the power of God's word.

In the paradise of the Garden of Eden, Adam and Eve are naked, but not initially embarrassed by their nakedness. Children are sure to giggle about this, so it is important to keep them focused on the story. You may want to explain that Adam and Eve are naked because at this point they are like babies being cared for by God. Just as babies don't notice that they're naked, neither do Adam and Eve. When they eat the fruit of *Eitz HaDaat,* they grow up very quickly, and part of what they learn about the world is that people wear clothes.

SYNOPSIS

After God finished creating heaven and earth, God creates a man from the dust of the earth. God gives him the name Adam (אָדָם), which means "earth." God places Adam in *Gan Eden* (גַּן עֵדֶן), the Garden of Eden, filled with beautiful trees and animals. In the center of the garden stands *Eitz HaDaat* (עֵץ הַדַּעַת), the Tree of Knowledge, the tree of good and bad. God tells Adam that he may eat from any tree except *Eitz HaDaat*. Eating from the tree will cause Adam to die. God lets Adam name all of the animals but sees that Adam needs a companion. While Adam is sleeping, God takes one of Adam's ribs to create a woman to keep him company. They are naked, but they aren't embarrassed. One day the *nachash* (נָחָשׁ), the snake, walks to the woman and talks to her, convincing her that she won't die if she eats the fruit from *Eitz HaDaat*. After she eats the fruit, she also gives the fruit to Adam. Now they realize they are naked and sew fig leaves together for clothing. They hear God in the garden and hide. When they tell God they are hiding because they are naked, God realizes they have eaten from *Eitz HaDaat*. God punishes them. God takes away the legs of the *nachash* so all snakes will always have to crawl on their bellies. God tells Adam and the woman that they must leave *Gan Eden*. Adam names the woman Chavah (חַוָּה). Because God loves them, God gives Adam and Chavah clothing from animal fur to protect them. God places two cherubim with fiery swords at the gate to *Gan Eden* to guard it.

DISCUSSION QUESTIONS

- Why do you think Adam and Chavah disobeyed God?

- Why did God punish Adam and Chavah?

- What are some of our family rules?

- Can you think of a time you didn't listen to your mom or dad? Do you think there should be consequences (something should happen) when you break the rules?

- Parents, when do you think it's appropriate to be inflexible (or flexible) with consequences?

RELATED ACTIVITIES

Make Your Own *Gan Eden*

Create a mural using a variety of different media. Cut pictures of animals and foliage from old magazines or wrapping paper. Draw your own pictures of the *nachash* (snake), Adam, and Chavah. Cut them out, and glue them to the mural.

Make a *Gan Eden* Mobile

Using heavy (card stock) paper, fashion a tree with fruit *(Eitz HaDaat)*. Punch a hole in the top, and attach a loop of string. Fashion a snake *(nachash)* to wrap around the tree. Draw and cut out Adam and Chavah. Attach a loop of string to each character, and attach them to the leaves of the tree. You may add animals too!

LESSONS 4 AND 5

Noah's Ark

תֵּבַת נֹחַ

Teivat Noach

Genesis 6:9–9:17

INTRODUCTION

Long after Adam and Chavah were sent out of *Gan Eden*, there were many people in the world. The world was full of violence and destruction, and the people were behaving very badly. Among these people, God selected the most righteous man, Noach, to carry out a plan to start the world over again.

There are many exciting related activities in this unit. You could spend at least two weeks on this unit.

SYNOPSIS

God decides, because the world is so filled with evil, that it needs to be started over again. All of the people and all of the animals will be destroyed by a great flood. Only Noach (נֹחַ), his wife, their three sons— Cham (חָם), Shem (שֵׁם), and Yefet (יֶפֶת)—and their wives will be saved. (In the Torah, the wives in Noach's family are not given names. Later on, the Sages gave Noach's wife the name Naamah [נַעֲמָה].) God instructs Noach to build a great *teivah* (תֵּבָה), ark. God tells Noach to take two of every animal, a male and a female, on the *teivah*. When people see Noach and his family building the *teivah* on dry ground, they laugh at him. The animals come on the *teivah* and are given special places to live. Soon, the rain starts. As it rains, the *teivah* is lifted up by the water. The people, the houses, and the animals are all covered by the water. It rains for forty days and forty nights. Noach and his family are very busy taking care of the animals. Soon after the rain stops, Noach sends out a raven to see if the water has gone down. Then Noach sends out a *yonah* (יוֹנָה), dove. The *yonah* circles around and comes back. Noach knows the water is still too high. A week later, Noach sends the *yonah* out a second time. The *yonah* flies around and comes back with an olive branch in its mouth. From this, Noach knows the treetops are beginning to show. The third time, another week later, Noach sends out the *yonah*, and it doesn't return. Noach knows the *yonah* has found a place to build a home and it is time to let the animals off the *teivah*. After all of the animals and people are off the *teivah*, Noach thanks God for saving their lives. God sets a beautiful *keshet* (קֶשֶׁת), rainbow, in the sky. The *keshet* is a sign of God's promise that, even though there will be natural disasters, never again will there be any reason for God to destroy the entire world.

DISCUSSION QUESTIONS

• How do you think people were behaving in Noach's time? How do you think they were treating each other?

- What qualities do you think Noach had that made him different from the rest of the people?

- Why did God save one male and one female of each animal?

- Think about natural disasters that you've heard about on the news: fires, hurricanes, tornadoes, and floods. How were people affected? Did the whole world get destroyed? Why not? Has God kept the promise?

RELATED ACTIVITIES

This lesson is rich in imagery and extended activities. Have fun with these suggestions!

Noach Mobile

1. Using heavy (card stock) paper, a paper plate, or craft foam, cut out a *teivah* (ark).

2. Fashion Noach and his wife from paper, and affix to the *teivah*.

3. Cut and color the outer 2-inch rim of half of a paper plate to create a rainbow.

4. Fashion several pairs of animals from paper or pictures from magazines.

5. Suspend these creations from a hanger.

Modeling Clay Animal Pairs

You'll need:

1 c. flour
1/2 c. salt
2 tsp. cream of tartar
1 T. oil
1 c. water
Several drops food coloring (or a package of unsweetened Kool-Aid)

Mix all ingredients in a pan. Cook over medium heat, stirring constantly. When mixture forms a doughy lump, remove from heat and cool. Put on disposable gloves and knead until smooth. Store in airtight container.

Combine primary colors and see what happens. Create animals using the modeling clay. Leave them out to harden when they're finished. Optional: Add a glossy coat of Mod Podge.

Fingerpaint a Rainbow

You'll need:

2 c. flour
2 packs unsweetened Kool-Aid
1/2 c. salt
3 c. boiling water
3 T. oil

Mix wet ingredients into dry ingredients. Use the mixture on glossy finger-paint paper.

Rainbow Stew

You'll need:

1/3 c. sugar
1 c. cornstarch
4 c. water
Food coloring

Mix the water, sugar, and cornstarch in a saucepan. Stir constantly until the mixture begins to thicken. Remove from heat and let cool.

Divide the mixture into three bowls. Add a different primary color of food coloring to each bowl. Put about three tablespoons of each color of the mixture into a reclosable plastic bag. Seal the bag. Knead the bag to mix the colors just enough to look like a rainbow. Lay the bag down on a hard surface and gently press to flatten it. You can hang it in your window when finished!

Animal Cookies

Make your favorite sugar cookie dough, or use the one in Appendix A. Cut dough into shapes using animal-shaped cookie cutters. Decorate with colored frosting.

LESSONS 6 AND 7

Tower of Babel

מִגְדַּל בָּבֶל

Migdal Bavel

Genesis 11:1–9

INTRODUCTION

The story of *Migdal Bavel* (מִגְדַּל בָּבֶל), the Tower of Babel, is actually a very short story at the end of *Parashat Noach*. However, this simple story provides an opportunity to teach about diversity, multicultural topics, family heritage, and important family values. We spend at least two weeks on this rich unit!

While the Torah does not mention King Nimrod, he is part of the midsrashic literature about this story and gives the story extra richness.

SYNOPSIS

After the great flood, Noach's family begins to increase, and eventually there are many people on the earth. They all travel together and finally find a suitable place to settle in the land of Shinar. They begin to build a town on the plain near the river. The king, Nimrod, wants his town to become a great city. He instructs the townspeople to build a great *migdal* (מִגְדָּל), tower, in the middle of the town. The people work tirelessly on the tower and begin to neglect their responsibilities to their families, livestock, and devotion to God. God sees this and confuses their language so they can no longer work together. Eventually, the people leave the *migdal* unfinished and leave their homes.

Legend tells us that people who spoke a common language traveled together and where they settled, a new country was established. For instance, people who spoke Chinese wandered and when they settled, they established the country of China. We get the word "babble," meaning "unintelligible speech," from the name of the city, Bavel (בָּבֶל).

DISCUSSION QUESTIONS

- Why did our family come to North America?

- How did our ancestors get here?

- What was their journey like?

- What foods does our family enjoy from other countries?

RELATED ACTIVITIES

Tell Stories

Tell some stories about your ancestors that might give your child a sense of your family heritage. Share old photos, songs, and family heirlooms.

In Your Community

Introduce your child to friends, neighbors, and family who may have recently come from other countries. Describe their unique clothing, foods, language, and customs. Emphasize the beauty of diversity.

Children around the World Mobile

On construction paper, draw the earth, and suspend it from a string. Draw children from around the world, or cut out pictures from magazines. Suspend these pictures from hangers, around the earth.

LESSON 8

Abraham and Sarah

אַבְרָהָם וְשָׂרָה
Avraham V'Sarah

Genesis 11:27–13:18

INTRODUCTION

This lesson initiates the study of the Matriarchs and Patriarchs (Mothers and Fathers) of the Jewish people. In the Torah, we first learn about Avraham (אַבְרָהָם) and Sarah (שָׂרָה) when they are already adults. The well-known story about young Avraham and the idols is a midrash, created long ago, to help us understand how Avraham may have realized there was one God. In the ancient city of Haran, Avraham lived among people who worshiped idols. The people believed that these statues of wood, stone, or metal had powers. They prayed to specific idols to fulfill their wishes.

SYNOPSIS

God says to Avraham (and Sarah), "*Lech l'cha*" (לֶךְ לְךָ), "Go!" God tells Avraham to leave his home and all the people he knows. God asks Avraham to travel to a far-off land. God promises Avraham that if he does what is asked of him, Avraham and Sarah will become the father and mother of a great nation of people. Avraham, Sarah, and their nephew Lot (לוֹט) pack their belongings, leave their home on a journey, and stop when God instructs them. They settle in the land of Canaan (כְּנַעַן). After some time, the workers who are taking care of Avraham's animals begin to argue with the workers who are taking care of Lot's animals. Avraham suggests that they each have their own land in order to end the quarreling. Lot agrees and moves his tents to the land near Sodom, while Avraham stays in the land of Canaan. Before going their own ways, they hug. God asks Avraham to look out over the land where he will stay, the land of Canaan. God promises Avraham that this land will belong to his descendants, the Jewish people, forever and that they will be like (as numerous as) the dust that covers the earth.

DISCUSSION QUESTIONS

- Describe what made Avraham and Sarah so special.

- In what ways do you think you or your family members might be like Avraham or Sarah?

- What are some reasons that people need to move away to another home?

- How did Avraham solve a family problem? Can you think of a time that a family member "gave in" to keep peace in the family?

RELATED ACTIVITIES

Conduct some research on the Internet or at the library. See if you can find pictures of nomadic people. Some people today live in tents that look like the ones from the time of Avraham and Sarah. What do their homes look like?

LESSON 9

Abraham and Sarah and Their Visitors

אַבְרָהָם וְשָׂרָה וְאוֹרְחִים
Avraham V'Sarah V'Orchim
Genesis 18:1–15 and 21:1–3

INTRODUCTION

Avraham and Sarah are now quite old (almost 100!) and have become well known in Canaan for their hospitality. Their tent was open on all four sides to let people know that they could come for learning or visits at all times. Avraham and Sarah are very happy in Canaan, but they are sad because they do not have any children and know that they are too old to have any. From this story, we become aware of the importance of *hachnasat orchim* (הַכְנָסַת אוֹרְחִים), hospitality to guests.

SYNOPSIS

One very hot day, Avraham is sitting in front of his tent, while Sarah is inside. In the distance, he sees three strangers walking toward the tent. Before the strangers arrive at the tent, Avraham gets up and goes out to greet them. He asks them to sit in the shade of his tree and offers them food and drink. Sarah prepares bread, and Avraham brings it to the strangers. They ask, "Where is Sarah?" When Avraham tells them she is in the tent, they say, "We are messengers (angels) from God. Tell Sarah, even though she is very old, she will have a baby." When Avraham tells Sarah the news, she laughs. She can't believe she'll have a baby at ninety years old! Months later, she gives birth to a baby, and they name him Yitzchak (יִצְחָק) which means "he will laugh."

DISCUSSION QUESTIONS

• What did Avraham and Sarah do to show hospitality to the strangers?

• The Torah teaches us to be kind to guests, but we need to be careful when meeting strangers. Discuss the difference between guests and strangers.

RELATED ACTIVITIES

Hachnasat Orchim—Hospitality to Guests

What can our family do to make guests feel welcome in our home?

• Help your child make a special welcome sign or picture to be used next time guests come to the house.

• Bake cookies for your next visitor. They can be frozen and be ready to use at any time.

• Invite guests over for Shabbat dinner, and involve your child in the preparations.

LESSON 10

The Binding of Isaac

עֲקֵדַת יִצְחָק

Akeidat Yitzchak

Genesis 22:1–19

INTRODUCTION

In this lesson, Avraham's faith in God is tested. God asks Avraham to sacrifice his son Yitzchak. When you sacrifice something, you give up something very special. In the time of the Torah, it was a common practice to make an animal sacrifice as a gift to God. God asks Avraham to do something that is very difficult.

The concepts in this story from the Torah are very sensitive and may be difficult for the young child to comprehend. Use your discretion when presenting the materials. When you do present the story, assure the children that God would never let Avraham actually kill his son.

SYNOPSIS

One day, when Yitzchak is a boy, God tests Avraham's faith. God asks Avraham to take his son Yitzchak up the mountain, build a fire, and sacrifice him as a gift to God. Early in the morning, Avraham and Yitzchak climb the mountain, carrying wood that they have gathered. When Yitzchak asks Avraham about the animal to be sacrificed, Avraham tells him God will provide the animal for the sacrifice. Avraham then places Yitzchak on a rock. As Avraham is about to sacrifice Yitzchak, an angel of God calls out, "Stop! Don't hurt your son. Now I know that you truly believe in Me." Avraham looks up and sees a ram caught in a bush. Avraham and Yitzchak sacrifice the ram, instead, as a gift to God. Because Avraham trusted in God, God blesses Avraham. God tells Avraham he will have as many descendants (the Jewish people) as there are stars in the sky and grains of sand on the ground.

DISCUSSION QUESTIONS

- What does it mean to have faith or trust in someone or something?

- In what or whom do you have faith or trust?

Note: Explain to your child that normally it is important to say "No" when someone asks you to do something that seems to be too dangerous or scary. Emphasize that in this story, God was testing Avraham for a very important job. Avraham was to become the father of all of the Jewish people. This was a huge responsibility, and God wanted to make sure Avraham was the right person.

RELATED ACTIVITIES

Use the library or the Internet to help your child understand the context of the story:

- What does a ram look like? Try: **www.desertusa.com/big.html**.

- What parts of the ram are used for something special? *(The horns are used to make a shofar.)* Can you find pictures? Try: **www.holidays.net/ highholydays/shofar.htm**.

- The land of Canaan is where the State of Israel is today. The rock where Avraham and Yitzchak sacrificed the ram is said to be the rock upon which the Temple was built in Jerusalem thousands of years ago. Find some pictures in books or on the Internet showing the beautiful Land of Israel and the city of Jerusalem.

LESSON 11

Eliezer Finds a Wife for Isaac

אֱלִיעֶזֶר מוֹצֵא אִשָּׁה לְיִצְחָק

Eliezer Motzei Ishah L'Yitzchak

Genesis 2:1–66

INTRODUCTION

Avraham is now quite old, and Sarah has died. Yitzchak will become the leader of the Jewish people and needs to find a suitable wife. Yitzchak's wife will help him lead the Jewish people and will be the mother of the future leader.

It may be interesting to tell the children that in the days of the Torah, men and women had distinct roles in family life and different jobs in running the household. The Jewish people were shepherds. The men and sons usually took care of the herding, and the mothers and daughters took care of the home. There was no running water, so the daughters were also responsible for gathering water from the *b'eir* (בְּאֵר), the well, and bringing it home. The well was also a place where people were able to meet each other.

SYNOPSIS

Avraham asks his servant Eliezer (אֱלִיעֶזֶר) to travel to the village where Avraham used to live to find a wife for Yitzchak. Eliezer asks Avraham how he will know when he finds the right woman. Avraham assures him that one woman will stand out as having special virtues. Eliezer takes his camels and travels to the nearby village. Upon arrival, hot and tired, he goes to the well, where the women are gathered. One woman, Rivkah (רִבְקָה), not only offers Eliezer water, but offers water to his camels as well. Eliezer knows that a woman who shows kindness to animals as well as to people will be the woman who should marry Yitzchak. Eliezer gives her gifts of gold jewelry. After meeting with her family, Rivkah agrees to leave her home and return to Canaan with Eliezer. As Yitzchak is working in the field, he sees Rivkah approaching. They fall in love, and Rivkah and Yitzchak get married.

DISCUSSION QUESTIONS

- The Torah places emphasis on the value of kindness to animals. What do we do in our family to take good care of animals?

- Eliezer was looking for special qualities for a wife for Yitzchak. What are the special qualities of your spouse, partner, or loved ones? Share your thoughts with your child.

RELATED ACTIVITIES

Kindness to Animals

As a family, do something special for animals in your home, environment, or world:

- Give *tzedakah* to an organization that cares for animals.

- Set up a bird feeder at your home.

- Decorate a special collar, bowl, or habitat for your pet.

LESSON 12

The Birthright

הַבְּכוֹרָה
HaB'chorah
Genesis 25:19–34

INTRODUCTION

Eisav (עֵשָׂו) and Yaakov (יַעֲקֹב) are twins born to Rivkah and Yitzchak. They are very different. Eisav is born first. Eisav will inherit the birthright. The idea of a birthright will be a foreign concept for the children. It would be easiest to explain that, in the time of the Torah, the oldest son became the leader of the family when the father was no longer the leader. In this case, the son with the birthright will also become the next leader of the Jewish people. You might have the children who are the oldest sons in their families raise their hands. Explain that this custom is no longer practiced and, in current times, women have the same privileges and opportunities as men.

SYNOPSIS

Some time after Rivkah and Yitzchak get married, Rivkah becomes pregnant. When she is pregnant, Rivkah feels her babies moving around a lot, as if they are fighting. When Rivkah gives birth to twin baby boys, Eisav is born first. He will inherit the birthright. Eisav is covered with hair and is very noisy. Yaakov is born while holding on to Eisav's heel. Yaakov is much quieter. As the twins grow up, Eisav likes to go off hunting animals, and Yaakov enjoys staying close to home, watching the sheep, and studying about God. One day, Yaakov is cooking a pot of red lentil soup. The wonderful smell of the soup beckons Eisav as he comes back from his hunting, tired and very hungry. Eisav desperately wants a bowl of the soup. Yaakov offers to trade the soup for Eisav's birthright. Eisav agrees to the deal, giving up his right to become the future leader of the family and the Jewish people.

DISCUSSION QUESTIONS

- Do you know a family with twins? Are the twins identical? Are they fraternal (not identical)?

- How were Eisav and Yaakov different? Can you think of people in the same family who like to do very different activities?

- Why do you think Eisav was willing to trade his birthright for the soup?

RELATED ACTIVITIES

Lentil Soup

There's a wonderful sensory opportunity when simmering lentil soup in your home. Here's a recipe to share with the entire family.

Lentil Soup

1 lb. dried lentils, rinsed and drained

1 medium onion, chopped

28 oz. can of plum tomatoes with liquid

1 c. shredded carrots (optional)

1 c. chopped celery (optional)

8 c. water

2 bay leaves

2 tsp. salt

½ tsp. pepper

Optional: herbs such as basil or oregano

Bring all ingredients to a boil in a large pot.
Simmer until tender, about 3–4 hours.
Remove bay leaves. Spoon the soup into
bowls. Enjoy!

LESSON 13

Isaac Blesses His Sons

יִצְחָק מְבָרֵךְ אֶת בָּנָיו

Yitzchak M'vareich et Banav

Genesis 27:1–28:9

INTRODUCTION

This portion from the Torah deals with very delicate issues. Not only do we deal with sibling rivalry, but also we experience a parent's apparent preference of one child over the other. On the surface, it appears that Rivkah shows favoritism toward Yaakov. With a deeper look, we see that Rivkah was concerned with the future of the Jewish people and made a very difficult decision to ensure the strong leadership of the Jewish people.

SYNOPSIS

Yitzchak is growing very old, is nearly blind, and feels as though he may not live much longer. He wants to bless his oldest son, who will take over as leader of the Jewish people. Rivkah hears Yitzchak tell Eisav to hunt for an animal and make the stew they enjoy eating, and that upon his return, Yitzchak will give him the blessing. Rivkah realizes that Eisav will not make a good leader of the Jewish people. Eisav does not love God the way Yaakov does. Rivkah tells Yaakov to trick his father and receive the blessing instead of Eisav. Yaakov reminds his mother that Eisav is hairy, while his own skin is smooth. Rivkah prepares the food and covers Yaakov's smooth arms with fur from an animal. Yaakov brings the stew to Yitzchak. Yitzchak questions Yaakov because his voice doesn't sound like Eisav's. As Yaakov comes closer, Yitzchak touches his "hairy" arms and is convinced that Yaakov is actually Eisav. Yitzchak gives Yaakov the blessing of the first son, and Yaakov leaves. Soon after, Eisav returns with his stew, only to find out that Yaakov has tricked Yitzchak, and Eisav can no longer receive the blessing. Rivkah learns that Eisav has vowed that upon the death of his father, Yitzchak, he will kill his brother, Yaakov. Fearing for Yaakov's life, Rivkah tells Yaakov to run away to the home of her brother Lavan (לָבָן) for safety.

DISCUSSION QUESTIONS

- What do you think Rivkah saw in Yaakov that she didn't see in Eisav? *(More devotion to God, more concern for other people.)*

- Yaakov will now become the leader of the Jewish people. What are the qualities of a good leader?

- Yitzchak was visually impaired. Do you know anyone who is visually impaired? How does he or she cope with his or her disability?

RELATED ACTIVITIES

Make a Stew

Eisav and Yitzchak loved to hunt and then eat stew together. Make a meat (or meat substitute) stew with your child. Enjoy it with the family.

Learn about Hunting

Investigate or discuss how people would hunt for their food in ancient times. What did they do with the animal skins? *(Eisav made clothing from the skins.)*

LESSON 14

Jacob's Ladder
סֻלָּם יַעֲקֹב
Sulam Yaakov
Genesis 28:10–22

INTRODUCTION

Yaakov has a dream about angels on a *sulam* (סֻלָּם), ladder. Later in his life, Yaakov will have another experience with an angel.

SYNOPSIS

Yaakov is running away from home and his brother Eisav. As night approaches, he becomes tired and decides to sleep by the side of the road. He takes a large rock to use as a pillow. After he falls asleep, he has a dream. There is a *sulam* from the ground up to heaven. Angels, *malachim* (מַלְאָכִים), are going up and down the ladder. God is standing at the top of the ladder. God tells Yaakov that the land will belong to him and his family forever. God also tells Yaakov that his family will grow to be very large and all the families of the earth will be blessed by his family. God assures Yaakov that he should not be afraid or lonely because God will always be with him, protect him, and bring him back to his home. When Yaakov wakes up, he says, "God was here and I didn't know it." Yaakov no longer feels afraid or lonely and realizes that this is a very special place. He calls the place *Beit El* (בֵּית אֵל), House of God. He places his rock by the side of the road as a sign to other travelers of God's goodness.

DISCUSSION QUESTIONS

• Do you remember a dream that seemed very real?

• How did you feel when you woke up?

• Did you ever feel that someone was talking to you in one of your dreams? What did this person say?

RELATED ACTIVITIES

Yaakov and the Angels

On construction paper, fashion pictures of Yaakov and several angels. Fashion a ladder from construction paper, toothpicks, straws, or craft sticks and glue. Cut out the objects, and suspend them from hangers to make a mobile, or make a diorama in an empty box from cereal, shoes, or tissues.

LESSON 15

Jacob Meets Rachel

יַעֲקֹב וְרָחֵל
Yaakov V'Racheil
Genesis 29:1–20

INTRODUCTION

Once again, we experience the *b'eir* (בְּאֵר), the well, as a critical meeting place for personalities of the Torah. The Jewish people of the Torah were shepherds and shepherdesses. Watering the sheep was a very important job. Later in the Torah, we learn how Yaakov becomes very wealthy because of his expertise in raising sheep.

SYNOPSIS

Yaakov finally reaches the village of his Uncle Lavan. As he enters the village, he sees the well with a large rock on top. Sheep are gathered by the well. Yaakov asks two men by the well if they know his Uncle Lavan. They answer, "Yes, and here comes his daughter Racheil (רָחֵל) getting ready to water her sheep." Yaakov lifts the heavy rock from the well and helps Racheil water her flock. He kisses her hand. Racheil is surprised, but Yaakov tells her that he is Rivkah's son (her cousin). Racheil brings him to her home, and Lavan greets him warmly. Yaakov meets Racheil's older sister, Lei-ah (לֵאָה). Lavan invites him to stay, and Yaakov works for him as a shepherd. Yaakov falls in love with Racheil. Lavan offers to pay Yaakov. Yaakov asks that he be able to marry Racheil instead of receiving money for his work. Lavan agrees, and Yaakov works seven years in order to marry Racheil.

DISCUSSION QUESTIONS

- Imagine yourself in the time of Yaakov and Racheil. How were their lives and jobs different from those of people today? How were they the same?

- Do you believe in "love at first sight"? What did Yaakov see in Racheil that caused him to fall in love right away?

RELATED ACTIVITIES

People in Love

- Tell your child how and where you met your life partner. Was it at a well?

- Compare your meeting with that of your child's grandparents or great-grandparents.

- Take out wedding pictures of the different generations and enjoy looking at them as a family.

LESSON 16

Jacob, Rachel, and Leah

יַעֲקֹב, רָחֵל, וְלֵאָה

Yaakov, Racheil, V'Lei-ah

Genesis 29:21–30

INTRODUCTION

What goes around comes around! Yaakov, who has been involved in deceiving both his brother and his father, is now tricked by his uncle/father-in-law, Lavan.

Lei-ah, Racheil's older sister, is often portrayed as being less physically attractive than Racheil. It is important that the children understand, however, that people should not be judged strictly on their looks and that people have many qualities that make them attractive. Additionally, it will be important for the children to know that in the time of the Torah, men could have more than one wife, and that marrying one's first cousin was common.

SYNOPSIS

After dutifully working for Lavan for seven years, Yaakov is now ready to marry Racheil. Lavan arranges a wedding and, unbeknownst to Yaakov, brings Lei-ah, covered in a heavy veil. In the morning, after the marriage, when it is light out, Yaakov lifts her veil and realizes he has been tricked into marrying Lei-ah. Angry at Lavan, Yaakov still wants to marry Racheil. Lavan agrees that he can also marry Racheil, but he will have to work for Lavan for another seven years. Yaakov's love for Racheil is so strong that he agrees to the deal. In the meantime, Yaakov learns to love Lei-ah and has several children with her. In all, Yaakov has twelve sons and one daughter.

DISCUSSION QUESTIONS

- Do you think Yaakov deserved to be tricked after the trick he played on his father? Would this be a nice thing to do in your own family?

- Talk about a time when someone in the family wanted something really badly and had to work very hard to get it.

RELATED ACTIVITIES

Working for a Goal

Just for fun, help your child think of something simple he or she would like. Set up a system or a chart for a period of time (perhaps a week) so your child can perform a task consistently in order to reach the goal. Along the way, point out how difficult it is to stay on task until you reach the goal. Can you imagine doing this for fourteen years!

The *B'deken*

In traditional Jewish weddings, before the actual ceremony, the groom actually checks to see if he is about to marry the right bride. This is called *b'deken*. This custom came about because Yaakov married the wrong bride. Why do you think this has become part of Jewish tradition? Can you find a picture, a video, or personal photograph of this custom?

LESSON 17

Jacob Becomes Israel

יַעֲקֹב נֶהֱיָה לְיִשְׂרָאֵל
Yaakov Neheyah L'Yisrael
Genesis 32:4–33

INTRODUCTION

Yaakov has been away from his home for twenty years. Lavan has given Yaakov a lot of his own sheep, and Yaakov has become a very successful and wealthy shepherd. God tells Yaakov to return to his homeland, but Yaakov knows that he needs to pass Eisav's camp along the way. He is afraid that his family may be harmed and is trying to make good decisions for the welfare of his family. On his journey, he prepares gifts to give to Eisav to appease Eisav's anger.* Yaakov brings his family to a safe place and sets up his own camp to be by himself.

*This lesson may be easily connected to the next lesson, "Esau Forgives Jacob."

SYNOPSIS

Yaakov is at his tent alone. He is very troubled about the safety of his family and cannot sleep. He gets up and paces in front of his tent. Suddenly, Yaakov is grabbed from behind by a stranger. He wrestles with the stranger all night, until the morning. During their struggle, Yaakov's hip is injured. Finally, Yaakov throws the stranger to the ground and holds him down. Yaakov realizes that the stranger is an angel from God. The angel asks Yaakov to let go. Yaakov says, "I won't let go until you give me a blessing." The angel answers, "You will no longer be called Yaakov; your name will now be Yisrael (יִשְׂרָאֵל), Israel, which means, 'One who can wrestle with God.'"

DISCUSSION QUESTIONS

- Have you ever been so troubled by something you felt like you were "wrestling" with it? With your family, discuss strategies and ways to deal with troubling issues.

- Think of a time you were really angry with a family member for a long time. Were you scared to face that family member again? What could you do differently in the future?

RELATED ACTIVITIES

Yaakov to Yisrael

Yaakov's name is changed to *Yisrael*, Israel. Where do we hear *Yisrael* or Israel every day? Why do you think that name was chosen for the Jewish state? Find some pictures of *Yisrael* (Israel), and share them with the family. Perhaps you have pictures from a trip to Israel.

LESSON 18

Esau Forgives Jacob

סְלִיחָה

S'lichah

Genesis 32:4–33:17

INTRODUCTION

Yaakov has been away from his home for twenty years. It is time to return home with his large family. He is scared to see his brother after all these years. This Torah story provides us with a wonderful opportunity to talk about forgiveness, especially among family members.

SYNOPSIS

Yaakov sends his servants ahead to see Eisav's camp. They report back that he has many soldiers. Yaakov is worried that Eisav is still angry with him for receiving the blessing of the first son. Yaakov sends his servants back to Eisav with gifts of animals, hoping it will make Eisav happy. The time finally comes for Yaakov to bring his family past the camp of Eisav. When Yaakov reaches Eisav, Eisav throws his arms around Yaakov and hugs and kisses him. They cry in each other's arms. Eisav is happy to meet Yaakov's family. Eisav forgives Yaakov. He tells Yaakov to pass by in peace with his family and hopes they both have successful lives.

DISCUSSION QUESTIONS

- Can you think of a time you were really angry with a brother, sister, or relative? How did you deal with the problem? Is there still a way to make things better?

- Why were Yaakov and Eisav crying? Have you ever cried because you were really happy? Describe the events.

RELATED ACTIVITIES

Family Reading

Read the book *Brothers* or another book from the bibliography about family or forgiveness. Discuss how important it is to be kind, truthful, and loving to siblings and family members.

S'lichah

The Hebrew word for forgiveness is *s'lichah* (סְלִיחָה). Jews have a special day every year when they ask for *s'lichah*. Can you think of that day? *(Yom Kippur.)* Discuss with your family why you think we take the opportunity each year to ask for *s'lichah* from God and from each other.

LESSON 19

Joseph's Coat of Many Colors / Joseph's Dreams

כְּתֹנֶת פַּסִּים
K'tonet Pasim
Genesis 37:1–11

INTRODUCTION

Yaakov has returned to Canaan with his wives, children, servants, and animals. His wife Racheil has died while giving birth to her second son, Binyamin. Yitzchak has also died, and Yaakov is now the leader of the Jewish people.

In this story, we deal with some very powerful emotions. Yaakov certainly loves all of his children very much, but he has a special feeling for Yoseif (יוֹסֵף), Racheil's first child. Yoseif reminds him of his beloved Racheil. Much to the dismay of the brothers, Yaakov shows favoritism to Yoseif. The brothers are jealous of their father's extra attention to this "special" child. Furthermore, Yoseif is boastful about having dreams that will predict events of the future. There are many highly charged emotions in the whole saga of Yoseif's life. This will set the stage for many interesting discussions. In relating to the children that Yaakov loved Yoseif more than the other brothers (or showed him favoritism), explain that this is not the way parents should generally behave. In future lessons, they will learn that God has special plans for Yoseif and that everything in Yoseif's life will happen for a special reason.

SYNOPSIS

After moving back to Canaan, Yaakov settles down with his family and establishes his home again. Yaakov is now the leader of the Jewish people. One day, Yaakov returns to his family with a beautiful *k'tonet pasim* (כְּתֹנֶת פַּסִּים), a coat of many beautiful colors, for Yoseif only. The brothers become very jealous of their brother Yoseif when Yaakov gives the coat to Yoseif. Making them even angrier, Yoseif tells his brothers of a dream in which he and his brothers were preparing sheaves of wheat in the field. Yoseif's sheaf stood up and all of the other eleven sheaves bowed down to his. The brothers asked him, "Do you mean that you'll rule over us someday?" Then, Yoseif told them of another dream. The sun, the moon, and the stars were bowing down to him. His brothers asked, "Do you mean that your father, your mother, and your brothers will bow down to you?" This was too much for the brothers to bear and they hated Yoseif.

DISCUSSION QUESTIONS

- It is important to feel that we all have special qualities. How does it make you feel when people brag about their toys, clothing, or special qualities?

- What qualities make you feel special?

- Did you ever have a dream that seemed very real? Tell about it.

RELATED ACTIVITIES

Yoseif Mobile

1. Fashion a picture of Yoseif. On plain paper, draw and cut out a form for Yoseif.

2. Cut strips of paper from colorful pictures in a magazine. Arrange them in stripes to form a *k'tonet pasim*.

3. Glue yarn for hair. Add features with markers.

4. Using metallic paper or foil, cut out stars, the sun, and the moon.

5. Suspend artwork from strings.

6. Attach at different lengths to hangers and enjoy.

LESSON 20

Joseph Is Thrown in the Pit / Joseph Goes to Egypt

יוֹסֵף בְּמִצְרָיִם

Yoseif B'Mitzrayim

Genesis 37:12–36

INTRODUCTION

In this lesson, we deal with very serious emotions. Yoseif's brothers are so angry with him that they want to kill him so they can be rid of him. At the last minute, they listen to one of the brothers, who decides that it would be terrible if they were to carry out their plans.

Once again, Yaakov is involved in a terrible "trick." In order to get rid of Yoseif, the brothers decide to play a heartbreaking trick on their father. They sell Yoseif into slavery. It is important to tell the children that, in the time of the Torah, people could be bought and sold as slaves. (When teaching about Pesach, this scene will explain how the Jews ended up in Egypt. They will remain in Egypt for many years. During the time of Moses, they will all become slaves.)

Paroh (פַּרְעֹה), Pharoah, is the king of Egypt. At this time, there is no problem between *Paroh* and the Jews. This is also a different *paroh* than the one in the story of Mosheh (מֹשֶׁה), Moses. These events occur about 400 years before Mosheh.

SYNOPSIS

One day, Yoseif's brothers are out in the pasture taking care of the sheep. Yaakov sends Yoseif to see how they are. As they see him approaching, the brothers decide they should kill Yoseif, throw him in a *bor* (בּוֹר), pit, and say that a wild beast ate him. Then they won't have to listen to his dreams! Their oldest brother, Reuven, says, "We cannot kill him!" So, they take Yoseif's coat off and throw him in the pit while they decide his fate.

The brothers notice a caravan of *Yishmaeilim* (יִשְׁמְעֵאלִים), Ishmaelites, passing by. (The Ishmaelites were a group of people from a neighboring area.) They sell Yoseif to the Ishmaelites, who will be traveling on their camels to *Mitzrayim* (מִצְרַיִם), Egypt. In *Mitzrayim*, the Ishmaelites will sell Yoseif as a slave. The brothers then dip Yoseif's coat in the blood of a goat and bring the coat to their father. They tell Yaakov that Yoseif was killed by a wild animal. Yaakov is heartbroken and mourns for his son Yoseif.

DISCUSSION QUESTIONS

- How do we solve problems in our family when one person gets angry with another family member?

- Is it nice to play a trick on your parents? Children, how would you feel if you made one of your parents very sad because you played a trick? Parents, how would you feel if you were tricked?

RELATED ACTIVITIES

Camels

Search in the library or on the Internet for "camel caravans." See what the caravan of Ishmaelites may have looked like. (Try **www.nabataea.net/ camel.html**, **www.kinneret.co.il/holyland/camel.htm**, or **www.rc.net/wcc/ israel/camel.htm**.)

From travel brochures or magazines, cut out pictures of people riding camels. Attach them in sequence to make a caravan.

Family Conflicts

Discuss a plan for telling someone in your family if you are very upset with him or her. Role-play to practice using your plan. Try to implement it next time there's a problem. Take the opportunity to reflect on your plan. Did it work or not? How could you improve it?

LESSON 21

Joseph Works for Potifar / Joseph in Jail

יוֹסֵף בְּבֵית הַסֹּהַר

Yoseif B'Veit HaSohar

Genesis 39:1–40:23

INTRODUCTION

In this lesson, we learn something about Yoseif's moral character. First, we learn that, even though Yoseif is a slave, he works very hard and is given a great deal of responsibility. Then he resists the temptation of a married woman, causing him to end up in the *beit sohar* (בֵּית סֹהַר), jail. While in jail, he tries to help his fellow men.

SYNOPSIS

Yoseif is brought to *Mitzrayim* and sold as a slave to a man named Potifar (פּוֹטִיפַר). Potifar is a very successful and important man. Potifar realizes that Yoseif is very capable and intelligent, so he puts Yoseif in charge of the entire household. He trusts Yoseif with all that he owns. Potifar's wife (her name isn't mentioned in the Torah) likes Yoseif a lot. She asks him if he would like to be her "boyfriend." Yoseif knows this is wrong and emphatically says "No!" each time she asks him. One day, when he is cleaning her room and no one is around, she chases him and pulls off his coat as he runs away. Potifar walks in as she is chasing Yoseif. Disappointed, she lies to her husband that Yoseif had actually chased her! Potifar is so furious that he has Yoseif thrown in the jail where the *Paroh* keeps his prisoners.

Some years after Yoseif goes to jail, *Paroh* becomes angry with two of the men who work for him. *Paroh*'s butler (who serves *Paroh* his wine) and baker are thrown into the same jail cell as Yoseif. Yoseif is given the responsibility of taking care of them. One night, both the butler and the baker have dreams. They tell Yoseif their dreams so he can interpret them. The butler tells his dream first. He says, "In my dream, there were three bunches of grapes in front of me. I squeezed them into *Paroh*'s cup and gave the cup of wine to him." Yoseif says, "The three bunches of grapes mean three days. In three days, *Paroh* will forgive you, and you will go back to your job serving wine to *Paroh*. Please, when you're free, tell *Paroh* that I am here, in jail, and can interpret dreams." Then the baker tells his dream. He says, "In my dream, I'm holding three baskets of bread above my head. There were birds eating the bread from the baskets." Yoseif says, "The three baskets mean three days. In three days, *Paroh* will have you killed." Three days later, *Paroh* sends his guards to the jail. Just as Yoseif had predicted, the butler is brought back to the palace to work for *Paroh* and the baker is killed. However, the butler forgets about Yoseif and does not tell *Paroh* about him. Yoseif stays in jail for another two years.

DISCUSSION QUESTIONS

- Why is it important to try your best at any job, even if you don't like the job?

- How should we treat people who may work for us in our home?

- Why do you think God gave Yoseif the ability to interpret dreams? *(Yoseif will use his special skills to help people.)*

RELATED ACTIVITIES

Make the Bread in the Baker's Dream

Find your favorite recipe for bread. Divide it into three loaves. Bake and enjoy! Talk about your dreams as you eat the bread.

Accepting Responsibilities

Like Yoseif, we are often given responsibilities for jobs or tasks that are important, but that we might not really enjoy. However, we must still try to do our best at these jobs. We learn from Yoseif to take pride in our jobs well done, even if we may not like the job. Are there jobs around the house that you need to do that you would rather avoid? What are they? Are you proud when you have completed these tasks, even if you didn't enjoy doing them?

LESSON 22

Pharaoh's Dreams

חֲלוֹמוֹת פַּרְעֹה
Chalomot Paroh
Genesis 41:1–43

INTRODUCTION

Yoseif stays in jail for another two years. His ability to interpret dreams not only saves his own life, but the lives of the inhabitants of an entire country and, ultimately, the Jewish people.

SYNOPSIS

One day, *Paroh* is troubled by two strange *chalomot* (חֲלוֹמוֹת), dreams. He sends for his magicians and wise men, but no one can interpret his dreams. Then, the butler remembers Yoseif and tells *Paroh* of his experience in jail. He tells *Paroh* how Yoseif had interpreted the dreams of the baker and himself and how the interpretations came true. *Paroh* sends for Yoseif to be brought from jail, and Yoseif appears before *Paroh*.

Paroh tells Yoseif of his dreams. He says, "In the first dream, I was standing by the bank of the Nile River. Out of the river, seven fat cows came to graze in the grass. Then, seven skinny and sickly cows came out of the river. The seven skinny cows ate up the seven fat cows, but they still looked skinny and sickly. In my other dream, I saw seven ears of fat and healthy corn growing on a single stalk. There were also seven skinny and shriveled ears of corn growing on one stalk. Then, the seven thin ears swallowed the seven fat ears of corn. No one can tell me what these dreams mean. Can you?"

Yoseif answers *Paroh*, "Your two dreams are actually one and the same. The seven fat cows and the seven healthy ears of corn mean that here in *Mitzrayim*, there will be seven years when there will be lots of food and good weather. The seven skinny cows and seven shriveled ears of corn mean that the seven good years will be followed by seven years of drought (no rain) and famine (no food). You need to find someone to supervise the collecting and storing of food during the seven good years. Then, during the seven bad years, this person will supervise the distribution of the food so the people of *Mitzrayim* won't starve."

Paroh says to Yoseif, "Since God has given you this ability to interpret the dreams, I want you to be in charge of overseeing this process. The only person who will be more powerful than you, in all of *Mitzrayim*, will be me. Here is my ring to show you how I trust you." *Paroh* also gives Yoseif a beautiful Egyptian robe and a gold necklace to wear as he takes charge of *Mitzrayim*.

DISCUSSION QUESTIONS

- How are dreams important in the Torah? What other people in the Torah learned from their dreams? *(Yaakov)*

- Have you ever had a dream that came true?

RELATED ACTIVITIES

Mobile of *Paroh*'s Dreams

Fashion and cut out pictures of *Paroh* and Yoseif. Fashion or find in a magazine and cut out pictures of seven fat and seven skinny cows. Do the same for seven skinny and seven fat ears of corn. Attach the pictures to string, and suspend them from two crossed hangers. Alternatively, you may affix the pictures to a large piece of paper to create a mural.

Modeling Clay Cows

Using modeling clay or homemade dough (see pages 19–20), fashion seven fat cows and seven skinny cows. Using a blue piece of fabric or paper for a river, place the cows alongside the river. Do the same for the corn. Make them funky colors!

LESSON 23

Joseph and His Brothers Reunited

יוֹסֵף וְאֶחָיו

Yoseif V'Echav

Genesis 41:44–42:38

INTRODUCTION

Just as Yoseif has predicted, there are seven years of plenty in *Mitzrayim*. During those years, Yoseif supervises the gathering and storing of the food in warehouses in the cities. A very large amount of food is collected. During this time, Yoseif marries and has two sons, Efrayim (אֶפְרַיִם) and M'nasheh (מְנַשֶּׁה). When the drought and famine occur, it affects all of the lands in the area. However, it becomes known that the people of *Mitzrayim* are not starving because they are receiving food from Yoseif. Many years have passed since Yoseif last saw his brothers. He is now a grown man, and he dresses as an important royal Egyptian leader. He no longer looks like the boy who was sold into slavery by his brothers.

SYNOPSIS

In Canaan, which is near *Mitzrayim*, Yaakov and his family are affected by the famine. Yaakov tells his sons to go to *Mitzrayim* to get food to prevent the family from starving. All of the sons, except Binyamin (בִּנְיָמִן), the youngest, go to *Mitzrayim*. Yaakov does not want to send Binyamin because he is the only remaining son of Racheil.

When the brothers arrive in *Mitzrayim*, they go to Yoseif, since he is the person who distributes the food. As they approach Yoseif, they don't recognize him, and they bow low to the ground. When Yoseif sees them, he recognizes them but acts like a stranger. "Where do you come from?" he asks. "From the land of Canaan," they answer. Yoseif accuses them of being spies. They reply that they are all brothers, born to the same father. They tell Yoseif, "We used to be twelve brothers. The youngest is back with our father, and one [Yoseif] is already dead." Yoseif says to them, "So, you **are** spies! Unless your youngest brother comes here, you will not be allowed to leave from here!" Yoseif then changes his mind and says that if one brother stays behind, the others may bring food back to their starving families, and when the youngest brother comes to *Mitzrayim*, Yoseif will allow them all to be free. The brothers start to argue among themselves, blaming this terrible fate on having "killed" their brother. They don't realize that Yoseif actually understands their language and turns away because he is crying. Unknown to the brothers, Yoseif gives his guards instructions to fill their bags with grain, but to return the money in each brother's sack. Shimon (שִׁמְעוֹן) stays in *Mitzrayim*.

When the nine brothers return to Yaakov in Canaan, they realize that they all have their money in their sacks. They are afraid that Yoseif will think they've been dishonest and that they really are spies. Yaakov will not allow the brothers to take Binyamin to *Mitzrayim* because he has already lost Yoseif and is not willing to lose Binyamin as well.

DISCUSSION QUESTIONS

- Why do you think Yoseif left the money in the bags?

- Why does Yoseif cry?

RELATED ACTIVITIES

What does a drought-stricken area look like? Can you imagine not having very much water? Visit the library or search on the Internet to find pictures of what it looks like when a land is afflicted by a drought.

LESSON 24

Jacob's Family is Reunited

יַעֲקֹב וּבָנָיו הִתְאַחֲדוּ
Yaakov U'Vanav Hitachadu
Genesis 43:1–47:27

INTRODUCTION

The famine in the land is very severe. When Yaakov's family finishes the food brought back by the brothers, Yaakov wants them to return to *Mitzrayim* for more. Y'hudah (יְהוּדָה) reminds his father that they cannot return to *Mitzrayim* without their brother Binyamin, and he takes responsibility for Binyamin's safety. As they prepare to leave, they take double the money in case the first money was left there by mistake, as well as gifts. Yoseif now plays a terrible trick on the brothers before revealing his true identity. In the end, we see how Yoseif forgives his brothers, believing that God had planned for all of these events to happen so Yoseif could save the Jewish people.

SYNOPSIS

The brothers, including Binyamin, return to *Mitzrayim*. They are afraid they will be in trouble for having the money from the first visit in their sacks. However, they are treated very nicely, and they are invited to Yoseif's home for dinner. Shimon is returned to the family. Upon seeing Yoseif, they once again bow to him, and give him the gifts they have brought. As soon as Yoseif sees them, he asks, "How is your father?" When Yoseif sees Binyamin, he is overcome with emotion and needs to leave the room to cry in private. When he returns to the dinner, he instructs his servant to fill his brothers' bags with food, put the money back in the bags, and put his silver cup in Binyamin's bag.

The next day, the brothers begin their journey back to *Canaan*. Just as they leave the city, Yoseif sends his servant after them. The servant stops them and tells them that Yoseif's silver cup has been stolen. He says to the brothers, "Why did you repay good with evil?" The brothers deny any wrongdoing and offer their bags for inspection. The servant searches their bags, beginning with the oldest brother and ending with the youngest. As planned, the goblet is found in Binyamin's bag.

When the brothers return to Yoseif's home, they plead for his compassion. Yoseif tells them, "Only Binyamin will have to stay behind as my slave. The rest of you may return to your father." Y'hudah pleads with Yoseif to let Binyamin return to their father and offers to stay in his place. Yoseif can't control his emotions anymore and asks for all of his servants to leave the room. Yoseif cries very hard and finally says to his brothers, "I am Yoseif whom you sold to Egypt. Don't blame yourselves for what has happened. God sent me here to save your lives from the famine." Yoseif is very anxious to see his father, Yaakov, and tells his brothers, "Now, go to Canaan and bring back your families and your animals. Bring my father back quickly." Yoseif sends wagons to make their trip easier. Yoseif hugs his brother Binyamin, and they cry together. He kisses all of his brothers as they cry with him and talk to him.

Yaakov and Yoseif are reunited, and they cry as they hug each other. Yaakov is very old and is grateful for seeing Yoseif again before he dies. Yaakov comes to Egypt with seventy family members. The family is given a special area of *Mitzrayim* called Goshen where they can live and raise their families and their sheep.

DISCUSSION QUESTIONS

- Yoseif was a very powerful man in *Mitzrayim*. He could have easily punished his brothers for being so mean to him. Instead, he forgives them and shows his love for them. What do his actions tell us about the emphasis the Torah puts on the importance of family?

- What do we learn from Yoseif about how to treat our family members?

RELATED ACTIVITIES

Read with your child the book *Brothers* by Florence B. Freedman, or another book from the bibliography about family or forgiveness. Discuss how important it is to be kind, truthful, and loving to siblings and family members.

LESSON 25

Jacob Blesses Ephraim and Manasseh

יַעֲקֹב מְבָרֵךְ אֶת אֶפְרַיִם וּמְנַשֶּׁה

Yaakov M'vareich et Efrayim U'M'nasheh

Genesis 47:28–48:22

INTRODUCTION

Yaakov has lived in *Mitzrayim* for seventeen years. He is now very old and wants to say his final words to his family. He blesses Yoseif's sons and asks Yoseif to promise that he (Yaakov) will be buried in Canaan with his ancestors. Yaakov blesses the boys by telling them that future generations will say, "May God make you like Efrayim and M'nasheh," which has become the very blessing parents use to bless their own sons before Shabbat, holidays, and special occasions. For daughters, the blessing is "May God make you like our mothers, Sarah, Rivkah, Racheil, and Lei-ah."

SYNOPSIS

When Yoseif is told that his father is very ill, he brings his two sons, Efrayim and M'nasheh, to Yaakov. Yaakov is very weak and sits up in bed. Yaakov tells Yoseif, "God appeared to me in Canaan and blessed me. God said the Jewish people would become a large community and the land of Canaan would be for the Jewish people forever." When Yaakov realizes that Yoseif's sons are with him, he asks that they come close to him so he can bless them. Yaakov hugs them and says, "Yoseif, I never expected to see you again. And now, God has even let me see your children as well." Yoseif brings his sons in front of Yaakov. Yaakov places his hands on the heads of Efrayim and M'nasheh. He begins his blessing by saying, "The God who has been the God of my fathers, Avraham and Yitzchak, the God who has been my God, bless these boys. May my name be remembered through these children, and may they be the fathers of many children." He then says that all Jews, *Yisrael*, will bless their sons with the blessing he will give them: *"Y'simcha Elohim k'Efrayim v'chi'M'nasheh,"* "May God make you like Efrayim and M'nasheh." Yaakov is able to face the end of his life knowing he has passed on a tradition from his fathers through himself and on to his grandchildren.

DISCUSSION QUESTIONS

- An interesting question arises here for parents and children. Yaakov, realizing he is about to die, calls upon two of his grandchildren, Yoseif's sons, to receive blessings. Why were Efrayim and M'nasheh chosen instead of Yaakov's sons? (Think about this before reading the answer!)

A popular answer from commentators of the Torah is that Efrayim and M'nasheh were the first set of Jewish brothers who did not fight, hurt each other, deceive each other, or promote ill feelings in the family. It is with this beautiful thought that parents bless their children today. There is no greater blessing than peace among brothers. Additionally, Jewish parents have prayed, throughout the ages, that their children should be able to withstand the temptations of the world around them and to build and maintain a strong, proud Jewish identity. Efrayim and M'nasheh were the first descendants of Avraham and Sarah to grow up outside of the tribe. While growing up in Egypt, they maintained their identity and didn't assimilate into the popular culture around them. This is another reason why we bless our children to be like them. May we all be blessed with proud Jewish children—and grandchildren.

- What virtues come to mind when we bless our daughters to be like the matriarchs Sarah, Rivkah, Racheil and Lei-ah?

RELATED ACTIVITIES

Bless Your Children

On Friday evenings or holidays, use the traditional blessing or create your own blessing to bless your child. What would you wish for your children? With what traits should they be endowed?

Frame for the *B'rachah*

Work together with your child to create a beautiful frame for a copy of the *b'rachah* for your children (page 84). Keep it handy to be used on Shabbat and holidays.

Birkat Y'ladim/Blessing the Children

FOR A BOY

יְשִׂמְךָ אֱלֹהִים
כְּאֶפְרַיִם וְכִמְנַשֶּׁה.

Y'simcha Elohim k'Efrayim v'chi'M'nasheh.

May God inspire you to live in the tradition of Ephraim and Manasseh,
who carried forward the life of our people.

FOR A GIRL

יְשִׂמֵךְ אֱלֹהִים כְּשָׂרָה,
רִבְקָה, לֵאָה, וְרָחֵל.

Y'simeich Elohim k'Sarah, Rivkah, Lei-ah, v'Racheil.

May God inspire you to live in the tradition of Sarah, Rebekah, Leah, and
Rachel, who carried forward the life of our people.

FOR BOTH

יְבָרֶכְךָ יְיָ וְיִשְׁמְרֶךָ.
יָאֵר יְיָ פָּנָיו אֵלֶיךָ
וִיחֻנֶּךָ.
יִשָּׂא יְיָ פָּנָיו אֵלֶיךָ
וְיָשֵׂם לְךָ שָׁלוֹם.

Y'varehch'cha Adonai v'yishm'rehcha.
Yaeir Adonai panav eilehcha
vichunehcha.
Yisa Adonai panav eilehcha
v'yaseim l'cha shalom.

May God bless you and keep you. May God look kindly upon you, and be
gracious to you. May God reach out to you in tenderness,
and give you peace.

LESSON 26

Baby Moses

מֹשֶׁה הַתִּינוֹק
Mosheh HaTinok
Exodus 1:1–2:10

INTRODUCTION

Four hundred years have passed since the time of Yoseif. At first, the Jews lived very peacefully in *Mitzrayim*. Each time a *paroh* died, his son would become the next *paroh*. For a long time, the *parohs* were very grateful to Yoseif for having saved the people of *Mitzrayim* from starvation. Eventually, there is a new *paroh* who doesn't know about Yoseif. This new *paroh* is afraid the Jewish population will grow too large. He is afraid that someday they might band together and fight against him. At first, he decides to make them slaves. The Jewish slaves are referred to as *B'nei Yisrael*, the Children of Israel (Yaakov's new name). *Paroh* forces the Jews to build the cities of Pithom and Raamses. Despite the rigorous work, the Jews continue to have many babies. *Paroh* orders that the mid-wives should kill all the Jewish male babies, but they do not. Then *Paroh* gives his soldiers orders that Jewish baby boys are to be drowned in the river Nile. The girls are allowed to live because *Paroh* can't imagine that the Jewish girls would grow up to fight against him. His soldiers keep track of the Jewish women who are expecting babies to make sure only the girls survive.

In this lesson, the children will learn how Moses escaped this decree and was saved by *Paroh*'s daughter. In the Torah, *Paroh*'s daughter does not have a name. In the Midrash, the great Sages gave her the name Batya (בַּתְיָה), which means "daughter of God." These great teachers felt that God must have had a role in placing her at the river's edge at the moment when she could save this child who would grow up to save the Jewish people. Additionally, it would be interesting to point out that, in the time of the Torah, all women had to nurse their babies. (Young children have generally seen a mother nursing her child.) Generally, only a woman who has recently given birth can nurse a baby. *Paroh*'s daughter had not given birth, so she was not able to nurse the baby.

This story begins the second book of the Torah, called Exodus or *Sh'mot* (שְׁמוֹת). This book describes the plight of the Jewish slaves in *Mitzrayim*, their flight from *Mitzrayim*, the wandering in the wilderness, and the receiving of the laws on Mount Sinai.

SYNOPSIS

Paroh's soldiers are ordered to kill all Jewish male newborn babies by drowning them in the Nile River. One Jewish woman, Yocheved, gives birth and hides her son from the soldiers. After three months, when she can no longer hide him, she makes a basket, covers it with pitch, and places him among the reeds near the riverbank. The baby's sister, Miryam, hides in the reeds to watch what will happen.

Paroh's daughter and her maids come to the river to bathe. *Paroh*'s daughter sees the basket and asks her maid to get it. When she opens the basket and sees the baby boy crying, she knows it must be a Hebrew child. Miryam approaches *Paroh*'s daughter and asks if she would like a Hebrew woman to nurse the baby. *Paroh*'s daughter agrees, and Miryam brings her mother. Yocheved takes the baby home, nurses him, and raises him. When he grows up, Yocheved brings him to *Paroh*'s daughter to live with her in *Paroh*'s palace. *Paroh*'s daughter names him Mosheh, which means "I drew (took) him out of the water."

DISCUSSION QUESTIONS

- One of the reasons *Paroh* was afraid of the Jews was that he didn't understand their customs and religious beliefs. If we don't know much about our neighbors or friends, what would be a good way to get to know them?

- What words would you use to describe *Paroh*'s daughter? Do you know other women who have these characteristics?

- In what ways do you think Yocheved taught her child about being Jewish?

RELATED ACTIVITIES

Using the Internet, library, or other resources, see if you can find pictures of ancient Egypt. Why do we know so much about how the ancient Egyptians looked? What do the reeds look like by the edge of the river? Bring in pictures or books to share with your classmates.

Try **www.ancientegypt.co.uk/menu.html**, or **encarta.msn.com/encnet/ refpages/RefArticle.aspx?refid 461511156**.

LESSON 27

The Burning Bush

הַסְּנֶה הַבֹּעֵר

HaSneh HaBo-eir

Exodus 2:11–4:18

INTRODUCTION

Mosheh has been nursed by his birth mother, Yocheved, and is now a prince in *Paroh*'s palace with his adoptive mother, the daughter of *Paroh*. He has not lived the life of the slaves, but he seems to have empathy for their situation.

While Mosheh is in Midian, *B'nei Yisrael* are miserable and cry out to God. God hears the cries of the Israelites and remembers the covenant (promise) with Avraham, Yitzchak, and Yaakov.

SYNOPSIS

When Mosheh grows up, he goes out among the slaves to see their hard work. He sees an Egyptian beating a Hebrew slave. He hits the Egyptian to make him stop, but he hits him so hard that the Egyptian is killed. He knows *Paroh* will kill him for this crime, so he runs away to the land of Midian. Mosheh stays in Midian and marries Tziporah (צִפֹּרָה), Yitro's daughter.

One day, Mosheh is tending Yitro's flock of sheep. The sheep wander into the wilderness, and Mosheh follows. Mosheh sees a bush that is on fire (הַסְּנֶה הַבֹּעֵר), but isn't being destroyed. Mosheh says, "I must turn to look at this marvelous sight. Why doesn't the bush burn up?" God calls to him out of the bush, "Mosheh, Mosheh." Mosheh answers, "Here I am." God tells him not to come closer and to take off his sandals because the place on which he is standing is holy ground. God says, "I am the God of your father, the God of Avraham, the God of Yitzchak, and the God of Yaakov." Mosheh hides his face because he is afraid to look at God. God tells Mosheh, "I have seen the struggle of My people in *Mitzrayim*. I hear their cries because of the Egyptian taskmasters. I know about their suffering. I have come down to rescue them from the Egyptians and bring them to a beautiful land, a land flowing with milk and honey, the land of Canaan." God tells Mosheh that he will be sent to *Paroh* and will ask him to free the Israelites from Egypt. When Mosheh expresses concern as to why he was chosen for this task, God assures him, "I will be with you." Mosheh is also concerned that *B'nei Yisrael*, the Israelites, won't believe that God spoke to him and won't follow him. God tells Mosheh to throw down his rod (stick). Mosheh drops the rod on the ground, and the stick turns into a snake. Mosheh backs away from the snake, but God tells him to grab it by the tail. As he does, the snake turns back into a rod. God tells Mosheh that this is a sign that God is with him, and when *B'nei Yisrael* see this, they will follow him. Mosheh is also concerned that he is not a very good speaker. How would he speak to *Paroh*? God assures him, "I will be with you and give you the words." God also tells Mosheh that he can bring his brother, Aharon (אַהֲרֹון), who speaks well. God will tell Mosheh, Mosheh will tell Aharon, and Aharon will speak to *Paroh* and *B'nei Yisrael*.

DISCUSSION QUESTIONS

• Why do you think Mosheh was so nervous about fulfilling God's request of going to speak to *Paroh*?

• Often, a parent asks a child to perform a task and the child responds, "Why me?" How does this compare to Mosheh's reaction to God's request?

RELATED ACTIVITIES

Everyone has moments when he or she is unsure if he or she can accomplish a specific task alone. Can you think of a time when your child needed moral, physical, or emotional support to complete a task? How was he or she helped? Perhaps you can use this as a personal example of Mosheh's concerns and worries. Your child may enjoy relating to Mosheh's dilemma.

LESSON 28

Moses and Pharaoh / The Ten Plagues

עֶשֶׂר הַמַּכּוֹת

Eser HaMakot

Exodus 7:14–12:42

INTRODUCTION

Mosheh leaves Midian and returns to *Mitzrayim* with his family. He meets Aharon and tells him about his encounter with God. Mosheh and Aharon talk to *B'nei Yisrael*, and they are relieved that God has noticed their suffering. However, *Paroh* is not as receptive to Mosheh and Aharon. In response to their plea, *Paroh* increases the workload of the slaves, making their lives even more miserable. God assures Mosheh that *Paroh* will let *B'nei Yisrael* go when *Paroh* realizes the power of the God of the Jews. Each time *Paroh* refuses to let the Jews go free, a terrible plague is brought upon the land, which affects only the Egyptians. After the last of the *Eser Makot* (עֶשֶׂר מַכּוֹת), the Ten Plagues, *Paroh* changes his mind.

SYNOPSIS

Mosheh and Aharon plead with *Paroh* as God commands, saying, "The God of the Jewish people sent us here to tell you, 'Let My people go so they may worship Me!'" When *Paroh* does not respond, Aharon touches his rod to the Nile River, and the water turns to blood. The Egyptians can no longer drink the water. After seven days, Mosheh and Aharon once again plead with *Paroh*. This time, when *Paroh* refuses, the land is covered with frogs. Mosheh and Aharon continue to plead with *Paroh*. Each time *Paroh* refuses, another plague is brought upon the Egyptians. Next, there is the plague of lice, followed by swarms of insects, then wild beasts, followed by a disease that kills the cattle. Then there are boils (painful bumps on people's bodies), then terrible hail, and then locusts that eat up all the plants and crops. The ninth plague causes several days of darkness. After *Paroh* can no longer put up with each of the plagues, he agrees to let *B'nei Yisrael* go free. Then, just as they're about to leave, *Paroh* changes his mind. Finally, Mosheh warns *Paroh* that the tenth plague will be the worst of all: the firstborn of every Egyptian family shall die.

In preparation for the tenth plague, Mosheh instructs *B'nei Yisrael* to kill a lamb and use some of the blood to put on the doorposts (frame around the door) of each house occupied by a Jewish family. The blood will let the Angel of Death know to **pass over** the homes of *B'nei Yisrael* on the night of the tenth plague so no Jews will die. In the middle of this terrible night, *Paroh* calls for Mosheh and Aharon and says to them, "Go! Leave *Mitzrayim*! Take everything with you including your animals! You are free to worship your God the way you want!" *B'nei Yisrael* leaves in such a hurry, they pack their dough before it has time to rise to bake it into bread. After this night, God asks *B'nei Yisrael* to remember this forever, by celebrating this event, Passover (Pesach), for seven days each year. During these seven days, Jews will eat unleavened (flat) bread, matzah (מַצָּה), to remember the bread that was not able to rise.

DISCUSSION QUESTIONS

- Using the example of Mosheh approaching *Paroh* ten times before he succeeds in his efforts, discuss with your child the importance of not giving up on a difficult task if he or she is not successful with his or her initial effort.

- Discuss special customs and rituals your family might have for Pesach (Passover).

RELATED ACTIVITIES

Ten Plagues Art Project

Cut pictures from magazines (or draw your own) that repesent the different plagues. Glue them to a large piece of paper, collage style, or create a mobile by gluing each "plague" to a small piece of heavy paper, attaching it to a string, and suspending it from a hanger.

Origami Frogs

Create origami frogs by following the instructions on page 96. Use these at the seder while reading the Ten Plagues.

Hint: The smaller your frog is, the farther it will jump!

A

Begin with a rectangular
piece of paper.

Step 1

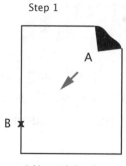

A

B ✗

Fold top right hand corner
so that point A meets
point B.

Step 2

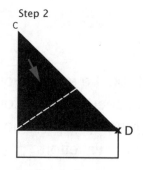

C

D

Now fold top left hand corner along
the dotted line, so that point C
meets point D.

Step 3

Open the paper
all the way

Step 4

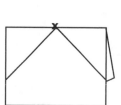

Fold paper in opposite
direction so that the
crease is at x.

Step 5

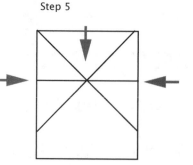

Paper should have creases as illustrated.
Push in the sides from behind.

Step 6

Push down the top triangle
along the creases.

Step 7

Fold the right and left hand
flaps (only the top parts) up
toward the point of the triangle.

Step 8

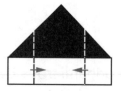

Fold in the sides
to the midline.

Step 9

Fold the top corners
in half and outward.

Step 10

E

Fold paper so crease
is at point marked E.
Now fold end of paper back so
that it forms a zig zag.

Step 11

Turn the piece of paper over.
Your frog is ready to hop.
Push down the back of your frog
at the place marked X.

LESSON 29

Leaving Egypt / Miriam and the Women

יְצִיאַת מִצְרַיִם / מִרְיָם

Y'tziat Mitzrayim / Miryam

Exodus 13:17–15:21

INTRODUCTION

There is perhaps no other event in Jewish history that holds such importance, excitement, and enduring meaning as *Y'tziat Mitzrayim* (יְצִיאַת מִצְרַיִם), the Exodus from Egypt. Because of its importance, we are reminded of the Exodus by making constant reference to this event in our daily prayers and in the *Kiddush* over the wine on Friday evening. Metaphorically speaking, all Jews were present at the Exodus, and subsequently at Mount Sinai.

SYNOPSIS

Through God's guidance and Mosheh's leadership, *B'nei Yisrael* flee from their homes in the middle of that frightful night, hoping that *Paroh* will not change his mind yet again, as they come to the shores of *Yam Suf* (יַם סוּף), the Reed Sea. However, when *Paroh* finds out that *B'nei Yisrael* have actually left, he can't believe he has lost his force of slaves, and he sends his soldiers on chariots to go after them. As *B'nei Yisrael* see the chariots approaching, they cry out to God and Mosheh. Mosheh tells *B'nei Yisrael*, "Have no fear! Watch the wonders God will perform to deliver us from slavery today." Then God tells Mosheh, "Lift up your rod and hold your arm over the sea and split it so *B'nei Yisrael* may walk through on dry ground." As Mosheh holds his arm over the sea, the waters separate and form a wall on either side of the dry land so *B'nei Yisrael* are able to walk through. As they reach the other side, they see the Egyptian soldiers coming close. God tells Mosheh, "Hold out your arm over the sea so the waters may come down on the Egyptian soldiers and their chariots." Mosheh does as God tells him, and *Paroh*'s army is swallowed up in the sea. When *B'nei Yisrael* see the wondrous power of God, they have faith in God and Mosheh. Then Miryam (מִרְיָם), the sister of Mosheh and Aharon, and all the women, take tambourines in their hands and dance in praise of God while Mosheh recites a song of celebration.

DISCUSSION QUESTIONS

- In their great rush to pack and leave *Mitzrayim*, the women didn't have enough time for their bread to rise, yet had the foresight to bring their tambourines with them. Why do you think they made sure to do this?

- In this lesson, we learned about wonderful miracles God performed. What are some miracles we see in our lives?

RELATED ACTIVITIES

What Would You Bring?

Take out several sheets of paper and markers for both the child and the parents. Fold each page in half. Pose the following questions: If you needed to leave your home in a great hurry and could only bring as much as you could carry, what would you take with you? Draw these items on one half of the paper. What would you leave behind? Draw these items on the other half. Compare the parents' papers with the child's paper, and discuss the similarities and differences.

LESSON 30

Mount Sinai / The Ten Commandments

עֲשֶׂרֶת הַדִּבְּרוֹת
Aseret HaDibrot
Exodus 19:1–20:18

INTRODUCTION

Finally free from *Paroh* and the Egyptians, *B'nei Yisrael* set out on their journey to the Promised Land. Little do they know that it will be forty years until the next generation is ready to enter the Promised Land.

Depending on the school and Jewish calendars, the teacher may want to present this lesson to coincide with preparations for the holiday of Shavuot when we celebrate the receiving of the Ten Commandments (עֲשֶׂרֶת הַדִּבְּרוֹת).

SYNOPSIS

Three months after they leave *Mitzrayim*, *B'nei Yisrael* enter the wilderness of Sinai. They set up camp at the bottom of the mountain. Mosheh climbs up the mountain to God, and God calls to him from the mountain. God tells Mosheh to tell *B'nei Yisrael*, "You have seen what I did to the Egyptians and how I brought you to Me. Now, if you will listen carefully to Me and follow My commandments, you will be My treasured people." Mosheh speaks these words to *B'nei Yisrael,* and they answer, "All that God has said, we will do." Mosheh brings *B'nei Yisrael*'s words back to God. God tells Mosheh, "I will come to you in a thick cloud so all the people will hear when I speak with you, and then they will trust you forever." Mosheh brings the people to the bottom of the mountain to meet God. The mountain shakes and smoke surrounds the top. God asks Mosheh to come up the mountain. These are the words that God says:

1. I am *Adonai* your God who brought you out of the land of Egypt, out of slavery.

2. You will not pray to any other god but Me. You will not make idols. You will not bow down to idols.

3. Do not ask God to do something bad to someone else.

4. Remember Shabbat and keep it holy. You may work for six days and do all your work, but on the seventh day you must rest.

5. Honor (listen to) your father and your mother.

6. Do not murder (kill).

7. Do not commit adultery. Keep your promise to love.

8. Do not steal.

9. Do not lie.

10. Do not be jealous of something your neighbor or friend has.

B'nei Yisrael learn to live by these rules as they continue their journey to the Promised Land.

DISCUSSION QUESTIONS

- Why didn't God give the Ten Commandments to the Jewish people at an earlier time, perhaps when they were slaves, or when they first left *Mitzrayim*? (Ponder this: When *B'nei Yisrael* were in Egypt, they were slaves and subject to the rules of *Paroh*. After crossing the Reed Sea, they are a new nation of people, on their own.)

- Why do you think the first commandment is a reminder of what God did for the Jews in *Mitzrayim*?

- Why do you think the second commandment reminds us to believe in only one God?

- Rules are important. What are some of our family's rules?

RELATED ACTIVITIES

Do a Mitzvah!

There are actually 613 commandments or mitzvot in the Torah. Different Jews understand the idea of commandments in different ways, but we can all strive to lead a life filled with mitzvot. Cut out a piece of paper in the shape of the tablets of Ten Commandments. Hang it where your child can see it. Each time your child performs a mitzvah, record it on this chart with a picture, sticker, text, etc. Include ritual mitzvot like lighting Shabbat candles as well as ethical mitzvot like honoring one's parents or being kind to animals.

Keep Shabbat

In the fourth commandment, God commands us to "remember the Shabbat and keep it holy (special)." Discuss with your family ways to make Shabbat special in your own home. (Some suggestions: Go to synagogue, bake challah, include the Shabbat rituals in Friday night dinner, invite company to share Shabbat dinner, sing songs after dinner.)

Appendix A
Recipe for Cookie Dough

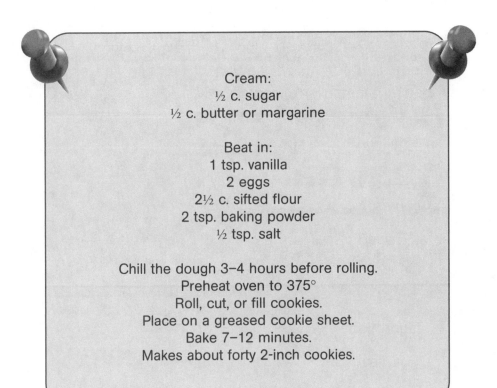

Cream:
½ c. sugar
½ c. butter or margarine

Beat in:
1 tsp. vanilla
2 eggs
2½ c. sifted flour
2 tsp. baking powder
½ tsp. salt

Chill the dough 3–4 hours before rolling.
Preheat oven to 375°
Roll, cut, or fill cookies.
Place on a greased cookie sheet.
Bake 7–12 minutes.
Makes about forty 2-inch cookies.

Appendix B
Useful Web Sites

www.urj.org/educate/ganeinu/index.shtml

The Union of Reform Judaism offers this online bulletin, *Ganeinu–Our Garden*. This publication addresses educational issues that concern Jewish early childhood programs. It offers discussion and insight to assist directors, teachers, and parents with the daily challenges of educating in early childhood.

www.urj.org/educate/childhood.shtml

The early childhood section of the URJ's Department of Lifelong Jewish Learning Web site includes resources and educational activities for the home and classroom. This site also includes parents' resources.

www.bjeny.org/434.asp?dept=Early%20Childhood&Programs_ID=111

This page from the Web site of the Board of Jewish Education of New York gives information about New York BJE's history with early childhood education, a description of its programs and instructions for how to become a member to access the BJE's resources.

www.kididdles.com/shop2/itm01972.htm

This is a for-profit site, offering for sale a variety of early childhood books, music, videos, and software. A site search using the word "Jewish" will yield many results.

www.jesna.org/cgi-bin/ilive.php3?op1=earlyc

The Jewish Education Service of North America (JESNA) is a non-denominational, Federation-based Jewish educational organization. It helps coordinate, plan, and develop Jewish educational initiatives throughout North America.

This section of JESNA's site offers an article about how to most effectively integrate Israel education into the early childhood classroom. The article discusses some of the challenges of much current practice, as well as suggestions for strengthening students' Israel learning.

Another section of JESNA's Web site (**www.jesna.org/cgi-bin/earlychild. php3**) includes early childhood education discussion groups, professional development programs, and an "electronic toolkit."

www.jafi.org.il/education/child/

Produced by The Early Childhood Division of the Jewish Agency for Israel and its Department for Jewish Zionist Education, this site offers a variety of resources: activities, curricula, and children's books (and their teacher's guides) for downloading; professional exchange opportunities; and projects, articles, and information on Jewish early childhood education. The site focuses on Israel education both inside and outside of Israel.

www.bjesf.org/ECEhome.html

The non-denominational Bureau of Jewish Education of San Francisco offers this useful site. It includes articles, information, Jewish texts, and terms for the educator's use. It also contains a discussion section for ECE professionals and a section serving the needs of the classroom. Each month's resources cover a new theme, such as a Jewish holiday or concept, and site visitors can access previous months' resources.

www.angelfire.com/fl/ajl/rainbowfish/presentation.html

Heidi Estrin, librarian at Feldman Children's Library of Congregation B'nai Israel in Boca Raton, FL, offers material at this site that she presented at the annual convention of the Association of Jewish Libraries. She presents a bibliography of secular children's books that highlight Jewish values. The site is conveniently arranged by value.

www.j.co.il/

This useful Web site contains a variety of practical Jewish learning resources and tools. The site includes a Hebrew sign-maker, a Jewish wisdom database, games, and clipart.

www.virtualjerusalem.com/

The bottom of this site's home page contains links to Jewish resources. These include stories, crafts, and a recipe archive.

groups.yahoo.com/group/cajeearlychildhood/

This is the Jewish early childhood educators' listserv from the Coalition for the Advancement of Jewish Education (CAJE). CAJE, the largest non-denominational organization of Jewish educators in North America, works to improve educators' and institutions' pedagogic and Judaic skills and the culture of Jewish education throughout North America.

groups.yahoo.com/group/jewishreggio

This listserv brings together a group of Jewish early childhood educators interested in creating and perfecting Reggio-inspired classrooms that effectively integrate secular subject matter with Jewish content, values, and Hebrew vocabulary.

www.jewishlife.org/pdf/autumn_2002.pdf

The Autumn 2002 issue of *Contact: The Journal of Jewish Life Network* focuses on Jewish early childhood education. The Jewish Life Network (also called the Steinhardt Foundation) is a philanthropic organization that aims to renew and revitalize Jewish life through educational, religious, and cultural endeavors.

www.meltonarts.org/artedu_lessonplans.php

MeltonArts is a project of the Melton Coalition for Creative Interaction. This coalition aims to promote Jewish learning through the arts. This section of the MeltonArts Web site includes lesson plans for teaching Judaism through art. To find lessons specifically geared toward early childhood settings, use the site's search engine to find "early childhood."

www.adl.org/education/miller/miller_printable.asp

This site contains a description of the Miller Early Childhood Initiative of A WORLD OF DIFFERENCE Institute—a project of the Anti-Defamation League. Aside from information about early childhood educator workshops, the site also lists some ways that educators can help students learn about diversity and coexistence skills. The Anti-Defamation League was established over ninety years ago in response to anti-Semitism in America. Now an organization that works against hatred and bigotry in all American communities, the ADL sponsors A WORLD OF DIFFERENCE Institute to help educate students and teachers for a diverse society.

jcca.org

This Web site is the electronic home of the national, non-denominational Jewish Community Center Association. The site houses JCCA's Early Childhood Education department, which features a theme-based preschool curriculum that follows the structure of the Hebrew calendar.

www.geocities.com/amynealw

A Jewish early childhood educator created this site to be an online community and source of resources for her and her colleagues. The site includes resource reviews, activities, ideas, and discussion groups.

www.torahtots.com

This colorful, fun site offers an Orthodox perspective on holidays and Torah texts. Based on a traveling children's performance, it features games, activities, coloring pages, holiday texts, and "Parsha on Parade," which includes a description of the week's Torah portion using a wide array of Torah-related Hebrew words.

Glossary of Hebrew Terms

Term	Hebrew	English
Adam	אָדָם	Adam
adamah	אֲדָמָה	earth
Aharon	אַהֲרוֹן	Aaron
akeidah	עֲקֵדָה	sacrifice
Aron HaKodesh	אֲרוֹן הַקֹּדֶשׁ	the Holy Ark
Aseret HaDibrot	עֲשֶׂרֶת הַדִּבְּרוֹת	the Ten Commandments
Avraham	אַבְרָהָם	Abraham
Batya	בַּתְיָה	Batya/Pharoah's daughter
Bavel	בָּבֶל	Babel
b'chorah	בְּכוֹרָה	birthright
b'eir	בְּאֵר	well
Beit El	בֵּית אֵל	Beth El
beit sohar	בֵּית סֹהַר	jail
Binyamin	בִּנְיָמִן	Benjamin
B'nei Yisrael	בְּנֵי יִשְׂרָאֵל	Children of Israel
bor	בּוֹר	pit
b'rachah	בְּרָכָה	blessing
B'reishit	בְּרֵאשִׁית	Creation
Canaan	כְּנַעַן	Canaan
chalamot	חֲלוֹמוֹת	dreams
challah	חַלָּה	challah

Term	Hebrew	English
Cham	חָם	Ham
Chavah	חַוָּה	Eve
Efrayim	אֶפְרַיִם	Ephraim
Eisav	עֵשָׂו	Esau
Eitz Chayim	עֵץ חַיִּים	Tree of Life
Eitz HaDaat	עֵץ הַדַּעַת	Tree of Knowledge
Eliezer	אֱלִיעֶזֶר	Eliezer
Eretz Yisrael	אֶרֶץ יִשְׂרָאֵל	Land of Israel
eser	עֶשֶׂר	ten
Gan Eden	גַּן עֵדֶן	Garden of Eden
hachnasat orchim	הַכְנָסַת אוֹרְחִים	hospitalty
hakafah	הַקָּפָה	parade with Torah
Har Sinai	הַר סִינַי	Mount Sinai
HaSneh HaBo-eir	הַסְּנֶה הַבֹּעֵר	the Burning Bush
keshet	קֶשֶׁת	rainbow
Kiddush	קִדּוּשׁ	Kiddush
k'tonet pasim	כְּתֹנֶת פַּסִּים	coat of many colors
Lavan	לָבָן	Laban
Lech l'cha	לֶךְ לְךָ	Go from here!
Lei-ah	לֵאָה	Leah
Lot	לוֹט	Lot
makot	מַכּוֹת	plagues
malachim	מַלְאָכִים	angels
midrash	מִדְרָשׁ	midrash

Term	Hebrew	English
migdal	מִגְדָּל	tower
Miryam	מִרְיָם	Miriam
Mitzrayim	מִצְרַיִם	Egypt
M'nasheh	מְנַשֶּׁה	Manasseh
Mosheh	מֹשֶׁה	Moses
Naamah	נַעֲמָה	Noah's wife
nachash	נָחָשׁ	snake
neirot	נֵרוֹת	candles
Noach	נֹחַ	Noah
ohel	אֹהֶל	tent
orchim	אוֹרְחִים	visitors
parashah	פָּרָשָׁה	chapter
Paroh	פַּרְעֹה	Pharoah
Potifar	פּוֹטִיפַר	Potifar
Racheil	רָחֵל	Rachel
rimonim	רִמּוֹנִים	Torah ornaments
Rivkah	רִבְקָה	Rebecca
Sarah	שָׂרָה	Sarah
Shabbat	שַׁבָּת	Shabbat
Shavuot	שָׁבוּעוֹת	Shavout
Shem	שֵׁם	Shem
Shimon	שִׁמְעוֹן	Simon
Simchat Torah	שִׂמְחַת תּוֹרָה	Simchat Torah
siyum	סִיּוּם	celebration
s'lichah	סְלִיחָה	forgiveness

Term	Hebrew	English
Sukkot	סֻכּוֹת	Sukkot
sulam	סֻלָּם	ladder
teivah	תֵּבָה	ark
tinok	תִּינוֹק	baby
Torah	תּוֹרָה	Torah
tzedakah	צְדָקָה	righteousness/ charity
Tziporah	צִפֹּרָה	Tziporah
Yaakov	יַעֲקֹב	Jacob
Yam Suf	יַם סוּף	Reed Sea
Yefet	יֶפֶת	Yefet
Y'hudah	יְהוּדָה	Judah
Yishmaeilim	יִשְׁמָעֵלִים	Ishmaelites
Yisrael	יִשְׂרָאֵל	Israel
Yitzchak	יִצְחָק	Isaac
Yocheved	יוֹכֶבֶד	Yocheved
yonah	יוֹנָה	dove
Yoseif	יוֹסֵף	Joseph
y'tziah	יְצִיאָה	exodus

Bibliography and Resources

CREATION

Creation: Books

Fisher, Leonard Everett. The Seven Days of Creation. New York: Holiday House, 1981.

Greene, Rhonda Gowler. *The Beautiful World that God Made*. Grand Rapids, MI: Eerdmans Books for Young Readers, 2002.

Greengard, Alison. *In The Beginning* (Hebrew and English). Oakland, CA: EKS Publishing, 2000.

McKissack, Fredrick, and Patricia McKissack. *God Made Something Wonderful*. Minneapolis: Augsburg, 1989.

Nerlove, Miriam. *Shabbat*. Morton Grove, IL: Albert Whitman, 1998.

Ray, Jane. *The Story of Creation*. New York: Dutton Children's Books, 1992.

Reed, Allison. *Genesis, The Story of Creation*. New York: Schocken Books, 1981.

Sattgask, L. J. *When the World Was New*. Grand Rapids, MI: Zonderman, 2001.

Creation: Music

Avni, Fran. "Once Upon A Time." *The Seventh Day*. Lemonstone Records, LSCD1003.

Glaser, Sam. "The Seven Days." *Kol Bamidbar: A Musical Journey through the Five Books of Moses.* Los Angeles: Glaser Musicworks, 1999.

Kol B'seder. "In the Beginning." *Songs for Growin'.* Transcontinental Music Publications 950077.

ADAM V'CHAVAH (ADAM AND EVE)

Howard, Fern. *Adam and Eve.* Leicestershire, England: Ladybird Books, 1990.

Hutton, Warwick. *Adam and Eve: The Bible Story.* New York: Macmillan, 1987.

NOACH (NOAH)

Noach: Books

Faulkner, Paul. *Two-by-Two.* Los Angeles: Price Stern Sloan, 1993.

Fussenegger, Gertrud. *Noah's Ark.* New York: J. B. Lippincott, 1982.

Geisert, Arthur. *After the Flood.* Boston: Houghton Mifflin, 1994.

Geisert, Arthur. *The Ark.* Boston: Houghton Mifflin, 1988.

Hayward, Linda. *Noah's Ark.* New York: Random House, 1987.

Hogrogian, Nonny (Illustrator). *Noah's Ark.* New York: Alfred A. Knopf, 1986.

Hollyer, Belinda. *Noah and the Ark.* Morristown, NJ: Silver Burdett, 1984.

Hutton, Warwick. *Noah and the Great Flood.* New York: Atheneum, 1977.

Lepon, Shoshana. *Noah and the Rainbow*. New York: Judaica Press, 1993.

Le Tord, Bijou. *Noah's Trees*. New York: Harper Collins, 1999.

Lorimer, Lawrence T. *Noah's Ark*. New York: Random House, 1978.

Ray, Jane. *Noah's Ark*. New York: Dutton Children's Books, 1990.

Reid, Barbara. *Two by Two*. New York: Scholastic, 1992.

Rouss, Sylvia. *The Littlest Pair*. New York: Pitspopany Press, 2001.

Singer, Isaac Bashevis. *Why Noah Chose the Dove*. New York: Farrar, Straus & Giroux, 1973.

Spier, Peter. *Noah's Ark*. New York: Doubleday, 1977.

Noach: Music

Friedman, Debbie. "The Rainbow Blessing." *Live at the Del*. Sounds Write Productions, SWP 607.

Glaser, Sam. "Two By Two." *Kol Bamidbar: A Musical Journey through the Five Books of Moses*. Los Angeles: Sam Glaser Musicworks, 1999.

Zim, Paul. *Zimmy Zim's Zoo*. Paul Zim Productions Inc., 1994.

Noach: Books about Colors

Ehlert, Lois. *Color Zoo*. New York: Harper Collins, 1989.

Ehlert, Lois. *Planting a Rainbow*. San Diego: Harcourt Brace, 1988.

Freeman, Don. *A Rainbow of My Own*. New York: Puffin Books, 1966.

Hoban, Tana. *Colors Everywhere*. New York: Greenwillow Books, 1995.

Hoban, Tana. *Is It Red? Is It Yellow?* New York: Mulberry, 1987.

Hoban, Tana. *Of Colors and Things*. New York: Mulberry Books, 1996.

Jonas, Ann. *Color Dance*. New York: Greenwillow Books, 1989.

Lionni, Leo. *A Color of His Own*. New York: Knopf, 1997.

Lionni, Leo. *Frederick*. New York: Knopf, 1967.

Lionni, Leo. *Little Blue and Little Yellow*. New York: Mulberry Books, 1995.

McMillan, Bruce. *Growing Colors*. New York: Harper Collins, 1994.

Munsch, Robert N. *Purple, Green and Yellow*. Buffalo, NY: Firefly Books, 1992.

Walsh, Ellen Stoll. *Mouse Paint*. San Diego: Harcourt Brace, 1989.

Noach: Books about Animals

Aliki. *Milk: From Cow to Carton*. New York: Harper Collins, 1992.

Barrett, Judi. *Animals Should Definitely Not Act Like People*. New York: Aladdin Paperbacks, 1989.

Barrett, Judi. *Animals Should Definitely Not Wear Clothing*. New York: Aladdin Paperbacks, 1989.

Bateman, Robert. *Safari*. Boston: Little, Brown, 1998.

Chessen, Betsey. *Animal Homes*. New York: Scholastic, 1998.

Esbensen, Barbara Juster. *Baby Whales Drink Milk*. New York: Harper Collins, 1994.

Gibbons, Gail. *Dogs*. New York: Holiday House, 1996.

Meadows, Graham. *Cats*. Milwaukee: Gareth Stevens, 1998. (Other animal titles available.)

Willow, Diane. *At Home in the Rain Forest*. Watertown, MA: Charlesbridge, 1991.

TOWER OF BABEL

Tower of Babel: Books

Greengard, Alison. *The Tower of Babel* (Hebrew and English). Oakland, CA: EKS Publishing, 2001.

Hirsh, Marilyn. *The Tower of Babel*. New York: Holiday House, 1981.

Mayer-Skumanz, Lene. *The Tower*. n.p.: Yellow Brick Road Press, 1993.

Weisner, William. *The Tower of Babel*. New York: Viking Press, 1968 .

Tower of Babel: Multicultural Books

Aardema, Verna. *Why Mosquitoes Buzz in People's Ears*. New York: Dial Books for Young Readers, 1975. (A West African tale.)

Anno, Mitsumaso. *All in a Day*. New York: Philomel Books, 1986.

Beeler, Selby B. *Throw Your Tooth on the Roof: Tooth Traditions from around the World*. Boston: Houghton Mifflin, 1998.

Brendon, Stuart. *The Children's Atlas of the World*. London: Grandreams Limited, 1993.

Brown, Marcia. *The Bun*. New York: Harcourt Brace Jovanovich, 1972. (A Russian tale.)

Chocolate, Debbi. *Kente Colors*. New York: Walker and Company, 1996.

Climo, Shirley. *The Irish Cinderlad*. New York: Harper Collins, 1996. (An Irish tale.)

Demi. *Liang and the Magic Paintbrush*. New York: Henry Holt, 1980. (An Asian tale.)

dePaola, Tomie. *The Legend of the Indian Paintbrush*. New York: G. P. Putnam's Sons, 1988. (A Native American tale.)

De Zutter, Hank. *Who Says a Dog Goes Bow-wow?* New York: Doubleday, 1993.

Ehlert, Lois. *Cuckoo*. New York: Harcourt Brace, 1997. (A Mexican tale.)

Forest, Heather. *The Woman Who Flummoxed the Fairies*. New York: Harcourt Brace Jovanovich, 1990. (A Scottish tale.)

Ginsburg, Mirra. *How the Sun Was Brought Back to the Sky*. New York: Macmillan, 1975. (A Slovenian tale.)

Hamanaka, Sheila. *All the Colors of the Earth*. New York: Morrow Junior Books, 1994.

Hofbauer, Michele Pace. *Couldn't We Make a Difference?* Bridgeport, CT: Greene Bark Press, 2000. (All children of the world working toward peace.)

Hurwitz, Johanna. *New Shoes for Silvia*. New York: Morrow Junior Books, 1993. (A Latin American story.)

Kendall, Russ. *Russian Girl*. New York: Scholastic, 1994.

King, Martin Luther, Jr. *I Have a Dream*. New York: Scholastic, 1997.

McClure, Herbert. *Children of the World Say "Good Morning."* New York: Holt, Rinehart and Winston, 1963.

Miller, J. Philip, and Sheppard M. Greene. *We All Sing with the Same Voice*. New York: HarperCollins Publishers, 2001. (Includes CD).

Montanari, Donata. *Children Around the World*. Hong Kong: Kids Can Press, 2001.

Morris, Ann. *Grandma Esther Remembers: A Jewish-American Family Story*. Brookfield, CT: Millbrook Press, 2002. (Others available in the "What Was It Like, Grandma?" series, including British American, Hispanic American, Chinese American, and Native American.)

Mosel, Arlene. *Tikki Tikki Tembo*. New York: Holt, Rinehart and Winston, 1968. (A Chinese tale.)

Polacco, Patricia. *Babushka's Doll*. New York: Simon & Schuster, 1990. (A tale of a Russian grandmother and her granddaughter.)

Simon, Norma. *All Kinds of Children*. Morton Grove, IL: Albert Whitman, 1999.

Sloat, Teri. *The Eye of the Needle*. New York: Penguin Books, 1990. (A Yupik tale.)

Snyder, Dianne. *The Boy of the Three-Year Nap*. Boston: Houghton Mifflin, 1988. (A Japanese tale.)

Spier, Peter. *People*. New York: Doubleday, 1980.

Stuve-Bodeen, Stephanie. *Elizabeti's Doll*. New York: Lee & Low Books, 1998. (A Tanzanian story.)

Surat, Michele Maria. *Angel Child, Dragon Child*. New York: Scholastic, 1983. (A Vietnamese immigrant story.)

Weiss, George (George David). *What a Wonderful World*. New York: Atheneum Books for Young Readers, 1995.

Tower of Babel: Multicultural Music

Conn Beall, Pamela, and Susan Hagen Nipp. *Wee Sing Around the World*. Los Angeles: Price Stern Sloan, 1994. (Recorded music with booklet of words and sheet music.)

Putumayo World Music: Musical adventures from many areas of the world.

Other suggested artists: Jack Grunsky, Ella Jenkins, Red Grammer.

AKEIDAT YITZCHAK—THE BINDING OF ISAAC

Cohen, Barbara. *The Binding of Isaac.* New York: Lothrop, Lee & Shepard, 1978.

YOSEIF

Yoseif: Books

Auld, Mary. *Joseph and His Brothers.* New York: Franklin Watts, 1999.

Kassirer, Sue. *Joseph and His Coat of Many Colors.* New York: Simon & Schuster Children's, 1997.

Lepon, Shoshana. *Joseph and the Dreamer.* New York: Judaica Press, 1991.

Murdock, Hy. *Joseph.* Leicestershire, England: Ladybird Books, 1985.

Pingry, Patricia. *The Story of Joseph.* Nashville: Candy Cane Press, 1998.

Williams, Marcia. *Joseph and His Magnificent Coat of Many Colors.* Cambridge, MA: Candlewick Press, 1990.

Yoseif: Music

Webber, Andrew Lloyd. *Joseph and the Amazing Technicolor Dreamcoat.* Chrysalis Records, 1982.

MOSHEH—MOSES

Mosheh: Books

Adler, David A. *A Picture Book of Passover*. New York: Holiday House, 1982.

Amery, Heather. *Moses in the Bullrushes*. London: Usborne Publishing, 1997.

Auld, Mary. *Moses in the Bullrushes*. New York: Franklin Watts, 1999.

Davies, Kate (illustrator). *Moses in the Bullrushes*. New York: Simon & Schuster Children's, 1996.

Hayward, Linda. *Baby Moses* (Step Into Reading). New York: Random House, 1989.

Hutton, Warwick. *Moses in the Bullrushes*. New York: Aladdin Books, 1986.

Lepon, Shoshana. *The Ten Plagues of Egypt*. New York: Judaica Press, 1994.

Nerlove, Miriam. *The Ten Commandments for Jewish Children*. Morton Grove, IL: Albert Whitman, 1999.

Pingry, Patricia. *The Story of Miriam and Baby Moses*. Nashville: Candy Cane Press, 2000.

Pingry, Patricia. *The Story of the Ten Commandments*. New York: Ideals Children's Books, 1989.

Topek, Susan Remick. *Ten Good Rules*. Rockville, MD: Kar-Ben Copies, 1991.

Mosheh: Music

Avni, Fran. *Mostly Matza.* Lemonstone Records LSCD1001.

Friedman, Debbie. *The Journey Continues.* Sounds Write Productions SWP614.

Kol B'Seder: *Songs for Growin'.* Transcontinental Music Publications 950077.

GENERAL

General: Books

Cowan, Paul. *A Torah Is Written.* New York: Jewish Publication Society, 1986.

Books Containing Stories about Jewish Values

Bogot, Howard I., and Mary K. Bogot. *Seven Animal Stories for Children.* New York: Pitspopany, 2000. (Respect, modesty, gratitude, honesty, attitude, friendship, responsibility.)

————. *Seven Animals Wag Their Tales.* New York: Pitspopany, 2000. (Helpfulness, making choices, cooperation, duty, teamwork, courage, accepting differences.)

Elkins, Dov Peretz. *Seven Delightful Stories For Every Day.* New York: Pitspopany, 2000. (Respect, modesty, gratitude, patience, hospitality, kindness, responsibility.)

Family: Books

Freedman, Florence B. *Brothers*. New York: Harper & Row, 1985.

Kalman, Bobbie. *People in My Family*. New York: Crabtree, 1985.

Kraus, Robert. *Herman the Helper*. New York: Prentice-Hall Books, 1974.

Morris, Ann. *Loving*. New York: Lothrop, Lee & Shepard Books, 1990.

Munsch, Robert. *Love You Forever*. Scarborough, Ontario, Canada: Firefly Books, 1987.

Williams, Vera B. *A Chair for My Mother*. New York: Greenwillow Books, 1982.

Forgiveness and Telling Lies: Books

Ganz, Yaffa. *Sharing a Sunshine*. New York: Feldheim Publishers, 1989.

Marshall, James. *George and Martha*. Boston: Houghton Mifflin, 1972.

McKissack, Patricia C. *The Honest-to-Goodness Truth*. New York: Atheneum Books for Young Readers, 2000.

Shannon, David. *No, David!* New York: Blue Sky Press, 1998.

Jealously and Envy: Books

Ganz, Yaffa. *The Story of Mimmy and Simmy*. New York: Feldheim Publishers, 2000.

Henkes, Kevin. *Chester's Way*. New York: Greenwillow Books, 1988.